Identity Crisis

Why the man in the mirror doesn't look like you, and what to do about it

By Lincoln Bain

Endorsements

"Lincoln Bain's story is an incredible one of hardship, tragedy, perseverance, redemption and triumph. According to the typical societal norms his destination should have been the prison or cemetery but through a series of miraculous interventions, personal determination and spiritual commitment, Lincoln has shown what is possible through faith and focus. I was blown away as I read through the pages and chapters: what an amazing journey that truly inspires and eliminates excuses for non achievement and failure."

Dr. Dave Burrows, BFMI
Successor to Dr Myles Monroe

"In this narrative, Lincoln grants his reader an 'All Access Pass' firstly to his own personal walk of purpose and then to the wisdom and experiences of one of the Kingdom's most outstanding Generals, Dr Myles Munroe. Once exposed to the supernatural battles that Lincoln Bain has himself overcome by God's grace, his journey to and with Dr. Myles Munroe is bound to leave the reader desiring more to be a true student and ambassador of the Kingdom and its Dominion mandate."

Ambassador Devon Rolle
Founder of ADR Worldwide & KDC International Embassy

"Amazing! Inspiring! One of the best books I have ever read! This writing is first class. When I was given the manuscript, I did not know what to expect but the more I read, the more I was inspired. This book will indeed go down among the best. I congratulate and applaud Lincoln Bain for this work. I fully endorse and recommend this book. It is a must read."

Dr. Carlos Reid
Founder of The King's Sons

"This is the most inspirational book I have ever read! Lincoln Bain's life story as depicted in *Identity Crisis* touches the heart and soul and entices the reader to pursue their dreams and fulfill their destiny. A powerful and life changing read!"

Cranston VG Evans
Author of Dropped But Not Destroyed

"A fascinating read! From the first page Lincoln Bain grabs the reader's attention and shows that he is indeed a true spiritual son of the late Dr. Myles Munroe with this new book on purpose and the Believer's identity. I recommend that you pick it up and let the author shake you out of your spiritual complacency, move you beyond your present 'identity crisis' and help you to find the purpose for which you were uniquely created!"

Pastor Lyall Bethel
Grace Community Church

"*Identity Crisis* is a treasure trove of wisdom and inspiration. It brilliantly illustrates that in order to find purpose you must find your identity. It is a concise and comprehensive guide to understanding your true identity and fulfilling your Kingdom Assignment in life."

Apostle Benjamin Smith
Pastor of Kingdom Training Embassy International

"This gripping personal tale of self-discovery, purpose and true success is a must read for every human. It will completely change your paradigm about who you are, why you exist, and why you do what you do. Its message is potent. You will find it both tough to put down and to ignore."

Simmone L. Bowe
Transition Strategist & Coach

"A convincing and powerful read! Lincoln Bain's *Identity Crisis* offers the reader an electrifying experience that compels him or her to explore their purpose and passion. Bain's expertise and experience is evident."

Duquesa D Dean
CEO of Duquesa D Dean Group of Companies, President of Transition Mentoring Program, and author of the book, Chase Your Dreams

"Purpose is a guiding light to personal fulfilment and an agent for generational impact. *Identity Crisis* by Lincoln Bain is a healing balm for your pain and disappointment, the fuel for your faith and the success manual that empowers you with the knowledge that you need to fulfil your dream according to your purpose. Lincoln's life is a miracle. The enemy of abortion tried to kill him in the womb but his purpose ambushed the plan of the enemy. *Identity Crisis* reads like a bestselling novel and an award-winning movie. It destroys low self-esteem with the power of hope and restoration. You were born to be great! *Identity Crisis* will help to release the greatness in you!"

Dr Debbie Bartlett
President/CEO
CEO Network Ltd, GEMS 105.9FM

Identity Crisis: Why the man in the mirror doesn't look like you, and what to do about it

Published by Dominion Media Publishing
http://lincolnbain.org/

Personal Growth, Self-Awareness, Christianity, Religion

Printed and bound in the United States of America by CreateSpace.

Cover, typesetting and editorial production by The Editor's Chair.

ISBN-13: 978-1537511931

Contents

Foreword

Are you a teenager staring into the future wondering what life will bring and which way you should go? Are you in your twenties and still struggling over how to choose the right career path? Are you in your thirties, tired of your mundane job and thinking that you should have accomplished so much more by now? Are you in your forties, divorced and wondering how to start all over again? Are you in your fifties and thinking that this is your last chance to find out who you truly are and to live the life you have always wanted? Are you in your sixties, regretting all the things you could have done and wondering if it is too late to change?

You are not alone. This is the greatest crisis on the face of the planet today. Billions of people on Earth are trying to find themselves and what they are here to do. As you will learn in this book, 70 percent of Americans hate their jobs. That is because so many of us are out of place. Walk into any office building and you will find that the lady at the reception desk is an imposter. She was born to be a Judge but due to circumstances she settled for any job that would pay the bills. Ride the elevator to the General Manager's office and you will find a man with a good paying job but yet feels unfulfilled. He was born to be a missionary but circumstances detoured him into a more lucrative direction. He, too, is an imposter.

In this life there is no greater tragedy than to not know who you are. All of mankind's short comings came as a result of not knowing who he is individually and who we are collectively. Can you imagine an Olympic track and field team where the skinny long distance runners are throwing the shot put; the heavy shot put throwers are attempting to run the 5000 meter event; the muscular short distance runners are running the marathon, and the discus throwers are running the 100m sprint? While this might seem like such an absurdity to even consider, the fact is that this scenario is being played out every day in real life. The question you must ask yourself is, "Am I a cook or a cleaner; a lawyer or a preacher; an athlete or a news anchor; an actress or a waitress?"

Identity Crisis will not only show you what went wrong but it will help you find yourself. Many persons tell you to live your purpose but they also fall short of telling you how. This book is a powerful, practical guide to how to find your purpose, and that of your loved ones. If you are ready to find your life, restart your life or change your life; if you are ready to transform into who you truly are, then this book is for you.

Introduction

It was an uncharacteristically cold and rainy day in the sprawling urban paradise of Miami, Florida. An old lady sat on a doctor's examination table as he removed the bandages from her left eye. Her right eye was so far gone that they had chosen to attempt to save the left eye first. For the past year she could open her eyes but see only darkness. Blinded by the scourge of men, diabetes, she had all but forgotten what it was like to stare into the sun, gaze up at the stars, or watch the waves on a beautiful beach roll and crash onto the shore. But today, after a number of surgeries, there was hope.

As she opened her eye her heart leapt with joy as her eye filled with light.

"What do you see?" the doctor asked.

"Light! Light!" she replied emotionally as tears began to flow down her cheeks. A few seconds passed and as her eyes began to come into focus she could see dark figures slowly taking shape.

"Now what do you see?" the doctor enquired.

"You," she replied, squinting her eyes as she struggled to bring them into focus. She could not really see him; she could only see a hazy outline in front of her. She began to focus on the other figure standing next to her doctor. Gradually the images were coming into view.

"What do you see?" the doctor asked again.

Her eyes flooded with tears. She lowered her face into her hands and began crying uncontrollably.

"What did you see?" the doctor enquired gently.

The old lady lifted her head and reached towards the image next to the doctor, pulling it towards her.

"What do you see?" the doctor asked one last time.

The woman replied, "My son."

The doctor was used to seeing people emotional about regaining their sight but there was something different about this one.

"What's the matter?" he asked. "Aren't you glad to see him?"

"You don't understand," she replied as she put her hand around the back of her son's neck and pulled him gently towards her. Then she pressed her forehead against his. "I tried to kill him, but he wouldn't die."

Almost thirty years earlier she was a twenty-four-year-old girl with two children fathered by two different men when she found herself pregnant again by another man. She had first gotten pregnant at the age of sixteen. As a result she was thrown out of her mother's house and left to fend for herself with the new baby. The child's father had abandoned her not long after she told him she was pregnant. Soon after she was pregnant again with a second child, the father also absconded. She struggled financially to raise them on her own for a few years. Now at the age of twenty-four she found herself in the same situation again – for the third time. She had to think about herself. She had to think about her two children. She had to let this one go. For the next few weeks and months she tried method after method to cause the baby to be aborted but nothing worked.

Then one day she was walking home with a bottle of pills clasped in her hand. These, a doctor told her, would definitely do the trick. She was determined to do what she had to do to save her life and those of her two young children. As she approached her doorstep a strange old Haitian woman grabbed her by the arm, startling her.

"What are you doing?" the woman asked in her thick Creole accent.

"Trying to get into my house," the young woman replied, pulling her arm away from the woman. She pulled away so hard that the bottle of pills dropped to the floor.

"The Lord showed me what you are doing," the Haitian lady said sternly.

"Please get out of my way," the young woman replied as she picked up her bottle of pills. "I need to get into my house."

The old lady stepped aside and motioned for the young lady to walk past her. As the young lady cautiously did so, the older lady began to quote a scripture.

"Before I formed you in the womb I knew you, before you were born I set you apart," she said authoritatively.

"What are you talking about?" the young lady asked as she pushed the key into her door to unlock it.

"What is inside you will bring light to your darkened eyes one day," the old lady replied. She grabbed the young lady's arm again. "What is inside you will travel the world and be seen by millions. Do not destroy what is inside you."

"Old lady, what are you talking about?" the young lady cried in frustration.

"Are you pregnant?"

"I am."

"Are you a Believer?"

"I am."

The old lady stood face-to-face with the young woman and held both of her hands. She then placed one hand behind the young lady's neck and pulled her closer until their foreheads touched. By now the young lady was crying.

"My dear," the old woman said quietly, "you have just said the most powerful words in the universe. You have just called on the most powerful force there is. When you understand the power of the name you just called on, you are safe, you are saved. Now go and sin no more."

The young lady went into the house, threw herself face down onto her tattered old couch and wept harder.

After hours of crying she sat up and stared blankly at the bottle of pills in her hand, her face awashed with tears. She, too, was an unwanted child. As a teenager her mother had been raped by a man she knew who had offered her a ride home from work. She was a virgin at the time and ended up pregnant.

Now she was torn. What should she do?

"What did you do?" the doctor asked as she recounted her story.

The old lady's face was drenched with tears, her forehead still pressed against her son's.

"I took the pills," she whispered.

She told the doctor that this son was the main person to have made the surgeries possible. He was the one who had travelled with her to seek medical help. As the old Haitian lady had said, this son had travelled the world ministering in word and song – appearing on the *Oprah Winfrey Show*, performing with Michael Jackson, and opening speaking events for Dr Myles Monroe. He had ministered on TBN, BET, The Word Network and INSP.

Sadly she was unable to see much of this as her sight had by now gone. But she had nothing to be ashamed of. Over the years she had turned out to be a great mother who had nurtured her son's gifts and made all of that possible.

When she told the doctor the name of the pills she had taken he turned to the son and said, "Son, I don't believe in a God but what I will say is that it's a miracle you're alive."

"I am," the son replied. "I am."

That lady's grateful son is the author of this book.

I am alive after surviving an attempted abortion.

I am alive after being declared dead from pneumonia at the age of four.

I am alive after breaking my neck in a car accident at the age of eight.

I am alive after being viciously stabbed in the chest twenty times as a rookie police officer by a criminal. The knife did not penetrate my skin – not once.

I am alive after a serious biking accident that left me with a broken back and briefly paralyzed. I was told that I would never walk again. Since then I have walked around the world declaring The Kingdom.

I am alive because of the principles in this book. I am alive because of what this life is for.

The most important day of your life is not the day you were born but rather the day you find out why.

Everything that was created has a purpose. Even the things we abhor or ignore on a daily basis were created for a specific reason. Every bird, bee or butterfly; every mouse, roach or caterpillar. Even germs and bacteria have a God-given purpose. Every creature has an invaluable contribution to make to this ecosystem we call Earth. It is not only the living that have purpose; even the dirt on the ground and the waters of the seas and lakes have a critical role to play. Everything that exists has a purpose. Nothing was created by accident – not even an unintended, unwanted child. Whatever your parents' marital status at the time of your conception, you are not an accident. You are a winner. You competed with 500 million other sperm in a race for the egg. You were a winner from the beginning. God saw that you were a winner from the start and as soon as you fought your way into that egg, He zapped you with the greatest trophy known to man: The Spirit of Life.

But this is not the greatest wonder on Earth. The most amazing thing is that of all of God's creations, man is the only creature that fails to fulfill his purpose. Ants carry out their roles without instruction and without fail.

Beavers build, birds fly and bees pollinate with precision. So how is it that man, the only creature made in God's own image, is the only creature that dies unfulfilled? It is because man is the only one of God's creatures that does not know his true identity.

A bee knows that it is a bee. It knows that it is here to pollinate, provide and protect. It knows that it can do all of these things. It knows that it is from the hive. Likewise a bird knows that it is a bird. It knows why it is here. It knows that it can hunt, fly, or scavenge. It knows that it is from the north; it is going south for winter and returning to the north in spring. Every living creature knows what it is and what it does. That leaves the one most critical question for all of mankind, both collectively and individually: Who are you?

Identity Crisis:
A feeling of unhappiness and confusion caused by not being sure about what type of person you really are or what the true purpose of your life is – Mirriam-Webster Dictionary

In this life there is no greater tragedy other than not knowing who you are. All of man's shortcomings have come as a result of not knowing who he is individually and who we are collectively. This is the root of all our flaws and failures. I think we can all agree that the world is in crisis. Every day in the media, on talk shows, in the news, and at the water cooler, we discuss the seemingly endless tidal wave of crises we find ourselves engulfed in as a people: War, Crime, Racism, Terrorism, Poverty, Abuse. For generation after generation, since time immemorial, there has been endless diatribe and pontification as to these seemingly omnipotent and omnipresent issues.

What I have discovered is that mankind's dilemma is not a crisis of War, Crime or Poverty. It is not a crisis of Racism, Disease or Abuse. Man's dilemma is a Crisis of Identity: An Identity Crisis.

If I know who I am I will be at peace. If I know who you are I will be at peace with you. If I don't know who I am, that is the ultimate poverty. If I don't know who I am then I identify myself with my external features. This is the root of all racism. When I know who I am I will not abuse my life or my talent. When I know who you are I will not abuse you, your life or your talent. When you know who you are your purpose is self-evident because it is inextricably linked to your identity.

It is indeed interesting that the word for being in a state of forgetfulness is 'amnesia'. In case you missed it: AM-nesia. Amnesia is described as simply not remembering and therefore not knowing who you are. The vast majority of persons alive today are suffering from this devastating ailment – not clinically, but spiritually.

As illustrated in the preceding story, before I was born my mother abused me. She abused me because she was in crisis. She was in crisis because she did not know her purpose nor did she know mine. When you don't know the purpose of a thing, you abuse and misuse it. You may be in the same situation today; finding yourself in a state of abuse and misuse. Not by another, but self-inflicted, simply because you do not know yourself. Each and every person on this planet is seeking to be somebody. The problem is they don't know who they should be because they don't know who they are.

Many motivational speakers and writers tell you to fulfill your purpose but fall short on guiding you as to how. How do you know your purpose so you can fulfill it? I have heard one author say that to find your purpose you have to go to your manual, which is the Bible. That is true but many of you have tried that and found that the Bible will tell you the purpose of mankind as a whole and it will tell you your spiritual role, but you don't quite see how it tells you what career to choose, which college to go to, or which city you should live in. As a result you are left lost and confused.

You are fired up and willing to fulfill your purpose but you simply don't know how. You don't know who you are or who you should be. You do not know why you are here. You do not know what you were placed on Earth to do.

Well, let me ask you: What happened to your childhood dreams? How did you get distracted from them? They were stolen right from under your nose. Now you see other people living your dreams!

There is so much you wanted to accomplish by now but you never knew where to start. How do you identify your purpose? How do you know what your gift is? And what about your children; how do you know how to guide them? How does a father know that his three-year-old son will be a golf champion and so guide him in that direction? What about the child with many talents; which one is the right one to pursue and encourage?

What about your 48-year-old co-worker in the mailroom who is such an amazing singer? Better than many of the superstars who have made millions. Now it seems that life and opportunity have passed him by. Is there still hope for him?

What about the young lady who was on such an amazing career path but fell in love with an abuser and ended up pregnant and mistreated and lost her career? Is there hope for her?

What about that young athlete who had so much promise but ended up with a career-ending injury? Is there hope for him too?

This book interweaves the personal experience of the Author and other well-known personalities such as Dr Myles Munroe and Michael Jordan with the stories of biblical characters like Joseph, Moses, and Adam and Eve to lay out the practical and compelling story of who we are and what we are doing here. In this book you will learn the enemy's greatest weapon and decode his timeless strategy for stealing identity and purpose. Once you know the strategy of the enemy, he is powerless against you.

The book goes on to reveal the paradigm shift from a life of laws to a life of purpose. Once the power and importance of purpose is established, this book will give you practical secrets to finding your purpose, finding who you are, and finding what you are meant to do.

This book has come into your hands, not by accident, but because it is time. It is time for you to Become. Despite your situation, despite your past, it is time for you to find out who you are and to find the courage to be that person. Notice I did not say to find out who you will be. You already are that person. You were born that person. It is time for you to make the person you are today match the person you were before you were in your mother's womb. You do not know yourself because you do not understand the mystery of the great I AM. Those three letters together form the most powerful words in the universe. If you understand them you will tap into a source so powerful that you will be able to achieve endless possibilities. You will be in a place of impregnable protection. You will live and be alive for the first time. You will experience life without end, life without limits, life without doubt, life without fear. You will experience the true source and meaning of life.

If you want more than a cubicle, more than a life trapped in an office plantation. If you feel you were meant to live for so much more. If you are ready to experience purpose and power. If you are ready to experience and understand the purpose and power that has been placed in you. If you are ready to discover your true identity, then this book is for you... Read on.

Chapter 1: The Devil's Secret Weapon

In 2002, I spent my nights sleeping on a thin bed sheet spread on the concrete floor of my abandoned family home. There was no furniture, electricity or running water. It was just me, the cold hard floor and my books. My first love was being on tour with my singing group, Vision. I had dropped out of college in order to make this happen so in the meantime I had to find a way to make ends meet until our careers took off.

I started selling shoes from the trunk of my old hatchback car to make a living. The business took off fast. The demand was so great that I had to quickly open my first store. On the day the store opened the crowds were overwhelming. The store front was overcrowded and there was a massive line just to get in. We sold out of shoes on the first day. We quickly expanded from one to four locations.

I began to find less and less time to focus on Vision, my first love. I would show up late then fall asleep during practice. To make matters worse, I decided to expand the business into other countries starting with Barbados, which was one of the farthest islands in the Caribbean from us in the Bahamas.

The business was a phenomenal success and made me a millionaire in my early twenties. I was definitely a success by most people's measure. I was able to move to one of the Bahamas' most exclusive communities called Paradise Island where the likes of Michael Jordan and Barry Bonds were property owners. I was able to drive a luxury SUV with a 32-inch TV and a beautiful wine bar. I was living the life I had dreamed of but it was not happening in the way I had dreamt it. Despite all of the apparent success I was a slave. I became a slave to the business and a slave to making money. Vision and our ministry became secondary to an ever-expanding business empire. I was stretched thin and felt unfulfilled. I started expanding into other businesses such as medical supplies, clothing, wedding planning – I was doing it all.

At the same time I went into TV production and started a TV show that became the most popular show in the country. My life had exploded from potential to smashing success in less than a year. Just a few short years earlier I had been patrolling Paradise Island as a police officer protecting its affluent residents; now I was one of them.

Yet I was unfulfilled. I was a success but I was a failure. I was a successful failure. The devil saw my dream of traveling around the world to minister in word, song and writing, so he distracted me with success. There is nothing wrong with achieving financial success but there is something wrong if it does not line up with your purpose. I was stretched so thin that I could not give Vision or some of my businesses the attention they needed and as a result some of them began to fail. The money I was chasing so adamantly was as elusive as the gold of El Dorado. In case you are unfamiliar with the story, El Dorado was the mystical city in South America, allegedly full of gold. The world's greatest empire of the day, Spain, went bankrupt trying to find it.

In the long run, the distraction cost me more than I could have imagined. There were songs and books that were never written, albums that were never released, and people that were not ministered to. I had gained the whole world but was losing my soul. It took me years to realize that I needed to repent, until an interesting life experience with my mentor Dr Myles Munroe transformed my thinking.

I was riding in a beautiful stretch limousine sitting opposite Dr Myles. Our limo was a part of a convoy including limos and a Rolls Royce. The limos, including ours, were filled with other pastors and ministers from near and far, but of course whenever Dr Myles was present he was the focal point. Not because he was an alpha male and not even because he was one of the wisest men on the planet, but because of this magical aura of love and acceptance that radiated from him. Dr Myles was always such a happy, warm, and welcoming person. He had a smile that could light up any room.

Moments earlier we had been in a mega church in Memphis, Tennessee. Dr Myles had delivered a powerful message on purpose. It seemed like every single person in the audience came up for the altar call. It was amazing. He prayed for and laid hands on what seemed like hundreds of them. After the service Dr Myles stayed in the area of the pulpit and greeted, talked to, had pictures taken with, signed autographs for, prayed for and blessed every single person who wanted to meet him afterwards. He never refused anyone. It was like he didn't know how to say the word 'no'.

Dr Myles had invited Vision to do a world tour with him. We would sing and he would speak. It was a beautiful synergy. So there we were after the service watching in awe as this massive crowd lined up to get a few seconds with Dr Myles. While this was taking place the organizers of the conference were worried that the restaurant they had arranged for dinner would close, and if it had not already closed they were worried that the food would be getting cold. But Dr Myles did his thing until the last person in the building had got him to autograph one of his books.

"Hold on to this autographed book tightly, young man," Doc said with his bright infectious smile. "It will be worth a lot of money one day."

They both burst into laughter.

Dr Myles continued, "There are many great books inside you and one day you will bring them forth and they will change lives, and many will seek your autograph as they are seeking mine tonight."

As Dr Myles finished, one of the organizers who had been standing there nervously for the last half hour, trying to get him to cut his after-service activities short, walked up and gently said, "Sir, the restaurant is waiting; we're very late."

"Then," Dr Myles said, as if about to give some deep sagely advice, "we'd better hurry." Again he burst into infectious laughter.

On the ride to the restaurant in the speeding limo, some of the persons travelling with us were offering Dr Myles board of director positions, business opportunities, invitations to join NGOs, to forward books – you name it, they were trying to get him to be a part of some of the great work they were doing. These were all great opportunities that any normal person would have taken with little consideration. But Dr Myles listened to one after the other and said no to all except one. I was astonished. Was this the same man who, moments earlier, had not been able to say no to hundreds of autograph and photo-hungry persons? For the past two hours it was as if the word 'no' had been foreign to him. Now it was like it was the only word he knew. I must have had a puzzled look on my face because in the middle of all of this Dr Myles smiled and gave me a wink.

Soon we were at the restaurant. We sat at a grand table that had been prepared for us. I was sitting opposite Dr Myles as dinner was being served. He looked at me and said, "So how are you doing, son? How do you like your first trip with me?"

I told him that I really appreciated the opportunity but I was confused about what had happened in the car. He had always taught us to live life to the fullest and maximize every opportunity but here he was rejecting opportunity after opportunity. I told him that all of those invitations he had been offered were good noble opportunities.

"And that is the problem, son," Dr Myles responded, confusing me further in the way he always did before he dropped a major revelation. "There is a difference between a good thing to do and the right thing to do."

The statement was so simple but when he said it, I fully understood its deeper meaning.

"The devil's biggest weapon is distraction," he said, leaving me hungry for more as he tucked into the contents of his plate and turned his attention to the entire table of people dining with us.

The Devil Made Me Do It!

That night I couldn't sleep. Dr Myles' words intrigued me. I stayed up all night in the hotel room searching the scriptures for every interaction the devil had had with humans. I found only three. It was interesting to see that there were not more encounters because we blame the devil for everything we do wrong. The understanding is that the devil tempted us and made us sin. But as I researched I realized that the devil was seemingly not interested in making us commit sins. He was not interested in making you lie, fornicate, or commit gluttony. He really doesn't care if you do those things. You lie because you are ashamed of people knowing the truth, or you are afraid of the consequences of people knowing the truth. You fornicate because of your own fleshly lust and desires. You are a glutton because of your own fleshly greed. "But every man is tempted, when he is drawn away of his own lust, and enticed" (James 1:14). As the Apostle Paul said, it is your flesh that is constantly at war with your spirit.

I realized that man's greatest objective was finding his purpose and fulfilling it. Therefore, the enemy's greatest objective is preventing man from finding his purpose and fulfilling it. Thus it is incumbent upon us to understand how the enemy operates so that we may defend against the wiles of the devil.

The Strategy of the Enemy

The devil is an experienced strategist and an efficient tactician. He sets his goals and executes them to the end. Sun Tzu, the great war strategist, said that war is the art of deception. Like all strategists Satan never attacks head-on and it is therefore extremely difficult to determine his goals based on his actions. He uses stealth so you never see him coming. He uses deception so you see him as an angel of light instead of the prince of the darkness. Depictions of the devil as a hideous, terrifying, red monster with horns are extremely deceptive. The devil would never come to you looking like that because you would either run away or be too terrified to listen to anything he had to say. Satan is an angel and he comes as an angel of light, not a hideous, horned monster.

In war, the keys to understanding the enemy's strategy are to observe his movements and to intercept his communications. The enemy's communications, however, are coded and near impossible to decipher. Therefore, one of the most important roles of a person in a war is that of the Codebreaker. Their purpose is to decode the communications of the enemy, to uncover their tactics and strategies. Likewise, we will uncover Satan's strategy by observing his movements and decoding his communications recorded in the Bible.

We have two perfect examples of the devil himself tempting persons directly in the Bible: Eve and Jesus. In one case the devil was successful; in the other he failed. By studying these examples, you will get a greater understanding of how the devil uses cunning strategy to separate you from your purpose, stealing your life by stealing your reason for being.

Decoding the Temptation of Eve

In the opening chapters of the Bible we see that Eve, the world's first woman, becomes Satan's first target for temptation. As the story goes, Satan, disguised as a serpent, approaches Eve and tempts her to eat the fruit of the one tree God had told them not to eat from. The consequence of eating from that tree would be immediate death. There is something very noteworthy about the devil's tactics here. Satan wanted Eve to eat the fruit, however he never told her to eat the fruit. Notice what he said in Genesis 3:4-5 after the woman told him that God had said that if you touch or eat of the tree you will surely die:

> "And the serpent said unto the woman, Ye shall not surely die: For God doth know that in the day ye eat thereof, then your eyes shall be opened, and ye shall be as gods, knowing good and evil."

There are three key things that the devil told Eve in that one sentence that changed the world:

1. **You shall become like gods, knowing good and evil.**
2. **Your eyes shall be opened.**
3. **You shall not surely die.**

Notice the devil never tried to get Eve to lie, steal, fornicate, blaspheme or do anything that we know to be a sin. These kinds of sins are of little interest to him. Likewise, you should also pay close attention to the fact that he also never told her to eat the fruit. Why wouldn't he just tell her to eat the fruit, if that was his objective? The answer is simple. If someone walks up to you and tells you to drink poison you would simply refuse. It is a stupid request. And this is why Satan chose to use the serpent to do his bidding. Think about it. Of all the animals in the world why did Satan choose to use the serpent?

Serpents at the time were not regarded as the hideous belly-crawlers that we see them as today. Additionally, you will recall, the serpent was the wisest and most cunning of all the beasts of the field. Therefore, the serpent would have had a reputation for being wise. Eve, of course, would have known of this reputation. Thus, the devil used the animal with a reputation for being wise to pass this information on to Eve.

Reputation is a key element of both trust and deception. Satan knew that Eve would trust information coming from the wisest of creatures. Once she took in the information she deceived herself by thinking that the fruit was good for food, good to look at, and good for wisdom (Genesis 3:6). Satan used the serpent to disarm Eve with the most powerful weapon known to man: The truth. Yes, you did read that correctly. Satan uses the truth to deceive us. That is not to say that he does not lie or that he is not the father of lies – he is. But he also uses the truth to deceive us. His favorite weapon is the truth, not lies.

If you take a careful look at the three statements he made, all of them turned out to be the truth. Firstly, he said you shall become like gods, to know good and evil. That turned out to be true as God confirmed this Himself: “Behold the man has become like us to know good and evil.” Secondly, the serpent said that man’s eyes would be opened. Again we see that this indeed did happen as their eyes were opened and they saw their nakedness. The last one was the key to the great deception. He told Eve that if she ate of the fruit she would not die. This seemed to be in direct contradiction to what God had stated. Yet despite the apparent contradiction, when Eve ate the fruit nothing happened. She didn’t die. It wasn’t until she gave it to Adam and he ate the fruit that their eyes were opened and the disaster took place. Adam was the key. The original instruction was for Adam. Eve eating the fruit was of no consequence. So Satan’s comments to Eve didn’t contradict God’s statement at all. The Apostle Paul made this clear in 1 Corinthians 15:22: “For as in Adam all die, even so in Christ shall all be made alive” (KJV).

Mankind died because of Adam eating the fruit. Likewise, we were saved because of Jesus dying on the cross. Had Peter or one of the other disciples, even John the Baptist, died on the cross, it would have had no consequence. Many persons died on the cross before and after Jesus did; two even died with him, just as Eve ate with Adam, but it was Jesus dying that made the difference.

Therefore Adam was Satan’s original target all along. So how did Satan manage to tempt Adam without saying a word to him? Satan understood that what you see is always more influential than what you are told. So he used Eve as a living testimony. So when Adam saw that Eve ate of the tree and didn’t die, he was convinced. It is kind of like the way we do marketing today; we see someone do something and they are successful, then people flock to do it too. So Adam was trapped in the same way that many people get ensnared into doing drugs and other dysfunctional activities: All your friends are doing it and they aren't dropping down dead. You see, Adam may have been more skeptical of the serpent's advice but there was no questioning the apparent authenticity of seeing Eve stand before him after having eaten the fruit.

So through the revelation of this great mystery, you can now understand that the enemy sometimes uses the truth to deceive you. Secondly, sometimes the enemy tempts you indirectly through those around you. By the end of this chapter you will understand why it is that you are being tempted in the first place.

Decoding the Temptation of Christ

The gospels teach us that Jesus was led into the wilderness to be tempted by the devil. So from this we learn that when you identify your purpose and you set out to accomplish it, you will be tested. Every product, service or concept is tested before it enters the market to ensure that it works and that it is worthy. Jesus was no different. So let's take a closer look at how the devil tempted Jesus.

You will notice that Satan never asked Jesus to do anything that was a traditional sin. He never tried to get him to lie, steal, fornicate or murder. He didn't tempt him with women or wine. In fact on the surface of it what he tempted him with were not sins at all. Satan's first request was for Jesus to turn stone into bread. It was not a sin to turn stone into bread. Actually Jesus later turned water into wine and that wasn't a sin either. So what was Satan's strategy in the three things he tempted Jesus with? Satan made three requests:

1. **If you are the Son of God, turn stone to bread.**
2. **If you are the Son of God, jump off the temple.**
3. **Fall down and worship me and I will give you all the kingdoms of this world.**

Now, I always thought the devil was tempting me when he sent a beautiful woman to seduce me into fornication or when he caused someone to make me angry so that I might lose my temper. Why didn't he try to get Jesus to fornicate or do some other sin? That is because he is not after getting you to commit sins. He is after your purpose. He knows that if he steals your purpose, he steals your life. To accomplish this, he attacks the first thing God gave us: Our identity.

Notice what he said to Jesus in the first two attempts: "If you are the Son of God..." He was attacking His identity, just as Satan used identity against Eve by saying that she would be like God. But Jesus identified Satan's more sinister plot. Firstly, this was not about turning stone to bread; this was about authority. For example, a car company owns the cars it produces. So if they crash a car with a dummy in it, that is considered a crash test. But if you walk into the car company one day and take one of the cars and crash it into a wall to test it, that would be considered unauthorized destruction. While both cars were crashed by a dummy, the second dummy had no authority to do so. Secondly, whoever you take instructions from becomes your ruler. Paul explained this in Romans 6:16 (NIV): "Don't you know that when you offer yourselves to someone as obedient slaves, you are slaves of the one you obey?" Jesus was therefore not about to take instructions from Satan.

But notice again how Satan used his favorite weapon, the truth, in an effort to deceive. Firstly, it is true that if you are the son of man you can turn stone to bread just like you can turn water into wine. Secondly, he used prophetic scriptures about the Messiah in his second temptation. The scriptures said that the Messiah would not have any broken bones. This is also true. Therefore if you are the Messiah, God will not allow your bones to be broken in a fall; He will send angels to carry you safely to the ground. However the problem here again is authority. The product does not have the authority to test the manufacturer – hence Jesus' response of "thou shalt not tempt the Lord thy God". Additionally, Jesus knew that just as God had allowed Adam to fail, that He would have allowed Him to fail. Think about it. Jesus went into the wilderness to be tested. If a manufacturer of a product is drop-testing it to determine its durability, he would not catch the product before it hits the ground and prevent it from breaking. That would defeat the purpose of testing it.

The last temptation was an interesting one. Jesus came to Earth to become King of kings and Lord of lords; to take dominion and rulership of the Earth for mankind. So what the devil did was appear to concede to Jesus. He offered to give it all to Jesus. Why take three years to do it when I can give it to you now? Why do it the hard way? Why have to worry about being tortured and dying on a cross? Just bow to me this one time then I will bow out and give it all to you. Again Satan was going after His identity and purpose: This is what You came to this world for. I have it. Let me give it to You.

It was true that that is what Jesus had come to this world for. It was also true that Satan had control of this world. The problem is that whoever gives you authority is your ruler. While Satan did have authority over the Earth, if Jesus had accepted authority from Satan, the act of acceptance would have given Satan authority over Him also. That would have been like the chauffeur feeling that he owns the car. Yes, the employer put him in the driver's seat, giving him control of the car. Yes, he has the authority to drive the vehicle. But at the end of the day it is the person in the back seat who is truly in control, not the driver. The universal fact is that if I have the authority to give you authority then I have authority over you; which includes having the authority to take it back. If a king makes you a governor over his lands and you accept the appointment then you are also accepting and confirming his authority over you. Jesus understood this principle. But Satan's main goal with his third temptation was to keep Jesus from the cross at all costs. The cross was the solution. So if he could get Him to die in some other way, by jumping off a temple or by attempting to fulfill His purpose in some other way, then Satan would win again.

As you find your purpose and are about to begin life's great journey, the enemy will attempt to distract you. He cannot steal your purpose so he will try to twist and distort it. He will bring fake people and opportunities into your life. One cannot stop a moving ship, but if you set it off course then you have defeated it.

In 1999 I met and became friends with a wealthy American guy on Paradise Island. He opened my eyes to the fact that I was out of place as a police officer. I took his advice and immediately started making plans to leave the police force and go to college. Almost immediately I started getting offers from senior police commanders to come and work for them in their respective areas. One of those offers was to become a police-recruit trainer and to thereby have an influence over every officer coming onto the force. I was still very young but the senior officer said she had seen something great in me from when I was a recruit. She felt that I would be a positive influence on future police officers. I refused all offers, informing them that I was going on study leave to go to college.

It was a difficult but easy decision that was later affirmed by something Dr Myles said to me in the airport in Bella Horizonte, Brazil. He told me how he had been one of the rising stars at the Ministry of Education, a government ministry in the Bahamas. He had started a small prayer meeting at his house and wanted to go full-time into Gospel ministry. The Prime Minister had seen his potential and wanted to make him the Permanent Secretary, which is the top non-political position in a government ministry. Myles walked away from that opportunity so that he could cultivate his small Friday-night prayer meeting into a global empire. Dr Myles said that if he had gone into politics he would have been good at it. He would have become Prime Minister of the Bahamas one day. But then he would have had influence over about three hundred thousand people on some small islands. Instead, he said, he rose to influence millions of people around the world.

Understanding purpose is the key to decision-making. When you understand purpose you understand your destination. When you understand your destination you can understand the direction you must take to get there. The Brazil conversation with Dr Myles helped me to understand his previous actions in Memphis. I now understood that in life there is good and evil but that in most instances both of these are the same. There are things you can do that are good things but if those things are not in line with your purpose, it is not right. In this life you were given one brain, two hands and 24 hours per day. Therefore distraction can be a fatal mistake. I now understood why it was so easy for him to say no to all those good opportunities being offered to him in the speeding limo. If they were not lined up with his purpose and would consume his most valuable resource, which is time, then it would be good, but not right. This is the key to righteousness. It is not only following the commandments but being guided by the great command on your life: The will and purpose of God.

At dinner in Brazil, Dr Myles made me understand why he could not so easily say no to the crowds of people who wanted to see him after the service in Memphis: This was his purpose. This was his mission. This was the very reason he was here on Earth. Everything else was secondary to this. It was almost 1.am and we were still at the dinner table. Dr Myles' entourage appeared noticeably exhausted and ready for bed but Dr Myles seemed so alert and alive like he was just getting started.

At one point Dr Myles leaned over to my singing group, who were at the table with him, and said, "Sons, your real ministry does not take place on the stage. It takes place after the sermon, after the performance. This is where you minister. This is where you build relationships and influence lives."

Most of Jesus' ministry was not behind a pulpit. It was at the well, at dinner, on the streets, touching people, changing lives. People *may* remember your speech but they *will* remember that close encounter with you. Those special words you said just to them or wrote in their book while autographing it. That special prayer you said to a husband and wife that keeps them together. That special affirmation you gave to a young man that gives him the inspiration that lifts him off his feet and propels him towards his dreams.

That last young man who Dr Myles autographed a book for in Memphis before being scurried off into the speeding limousine is the Author of this book.

The Enemy's Greatest Skill

Satan's greatest skill is the art of counterfeiting. Counterfeiters do not destroy money, they copy it. The difference between real and counterfeit money is authorization. While Christ used the truth to make us become alive, Satan uses the truth to make us become a lie. When you are not living for the purpose you were created for, you are living a lie. You are a counterfeit. One day you will come before the Great Banker in Heaven to be judged, and He will say He does not know you and discard you.

Purpose and life are like the indissoluble elements of water: H^2O. For water to exist these elements must become one. Once these two elements are joined to become water it is near impossible to separate them. And if you do manage to separate them, the water is no more. Your purpose is your life; without it you are no more. Therefore you should be careful to never lose your purpose, because if you lose your purpose you lose your life.

The enemy's strategy is to corrupt your life and purpose – make it undrinkable; make it unusable; make it muddy. And that is what he did in the parable of the wheat and the tares in Matthew 13:14-30. It says that after the farmer planted his wheat, the farmer's enemy came in secret and planted tares among the wheat. Jesus was showing you how Satan works. The enemy did not come and destroy the farmer's wheat. Why not? Because the farmer would just plant more. But if he planted a wheat counterfeit then the farmer would be deceived until it was too late. A tare plant is extremely difficult to distinguish from a wheat plant. You cannot notice the difference until they are both ripe and ready for harvesting. If Satan can make you become a counterfeit by inserting counterfeit elements into your life, then he wins. This was his plan of attack with both Eve and Jesus.

What makes a counterfeit a counterfeit? It is made of basically the same stuff as, and looks similar to, the original but you can distinguish it by a closer examination of its authority and identity. Satan used these two elements to tempt both Eve and Jesus and this is what he will do to you. He will use your impatience and ambition against you. You want success now so he will offer you the greatest opportunities in the world if you will bow to him. The process and mission are integral parts of your purpose. There are no shortcuts; your life is the long road to your destination. It is not just the destination. Therefore, the route you take to get there is just as important as getting there. Jesus came to take dominion of this world from Satan but there was an established process for accomplishing this, so if Jesus had veered from this process He would have failed.

This brings us to the final major revelation of this chapter. How exactly did Satan get this dominion in the first place, and why did he go after Adam's dominion?

How the Enemy Stole Dominion

To get a full understanding of how and why the devil went after Adam we must first understand where Satan came from. Satan is actually not his name. It is a title which means 'the adversary'. His name is Lucifer – the morning star. We learn this in Isaiah 14:12. Additionally Lucifer once was in Eden. The scripture says that he was in Eden, the Garden of God. We learn this in Ezekiel 28:12. This means that he was in the presence of God. This was when Eden was in Heaven, before God placed Eden on Earth and placed man in it. Satan lost his glorious position in Eden and was replaced by man in the delightful Garden.

I love Dr Myles Munroe's definition of Eden. He says that the word 'Eden' means the spot where, for the time being, there is a connection to God; it is a delightful place. Basically, we can break that down to say that Eden is the spot where there is a connection to God. Satan was jealous of man's new dominion and place in that pleasurable spot. He was hell-bent on doing whatever he could to get man out of that spot and steal his dominion.

We have all heard the story of how Satan tempted Adam through the serpent via Eve and got them out of the spot, Eden. What is hidden in that story is his greatest feat of all. Everyone says that Satan got dominion of Earth when man fell, but no one really explains how he did it. The answer is in the understanding of the principle of responsibility.

As young police officers we were taught early on that when you go to a scene you speak to the person in charge. Let's say there was a disturbance at a bank. When we got to the scene we did not speak to the janitor, nor did we speak to the tellers. We asked for the person in charge: the manager. The janitor is not able to respond to our enquiries because he does not have the authority. The teller does not have the ability to give us a response because she does not have the authority either. The only person with the ability to give us a response is the person with the responsibility and that is the manager.

Responsibility means 'the ability to respond', respond not only in a verbal sense; it also means 'to act'. So, in essence, responsibility means 'the ability to act'. God is a God of order. After Adam and Eve ate the fruit, notice who God sought out and questioned: the person He left in charge – Adam. He came to the scene of the crime and spoke to Adam. Notice what Adam did. He put the responsibility on Eve. Eve in turn put the responsibility on Satan. But notice what Satan did. He kept silent. You see, Satan understood one of life's greatest principles: when you blame something it becomes your ruler. Whatever you blame, you empower. You can't open that business because there is too much competition. You've just empowered the competition. You can't go to college because you don't have the money. You've just made money your master. While studying the Hebrew uses of the word 'blame' I came across something interesting. Blame was one of the uses of the Hebrew word *nathan*, which means 'to deliver', 'hand to' or 'bestow upon'. So, when you blame, you are handing over authority.

Take a careful look at what happened in the Garden. Adam passed the responsibility to Eve by blaming her. So then God who is a God of order spoke to Eve. Eve then passed the responsibility to Satan by blaming him. Satan kept quiet. He passed no blame. He didn't even say, "God, I didn't tell them to eat the fruit." He said absolutely nothing. So then, what did God do? God is a God of order so He spoke to the new person in charge, reversing the sequence. First He spoke to Satan in the snake suit, placing a curse on him to reduce his power while outlining the solution to the problem in the curse. Then He spoke to the woman, reducing the effect of their actions by stating that the man will rule over the woman. Finally God spoke to Adam. This is how man handed authority over to Satan. Satan did not steal it at all. It was given to him.

To whom or what are you giving dominion over your life today by passing the blame? Never blame anyone for your situation even if they wronged you. Today, we constantly blame the devil. Every time we sin we say it was the devil, thus empowering him over our lives. So not only are we distracted but we are blaming the thing that distracted us, further empowering it over our lives. Interestingly, the word 'blame' comes from the Latin word *blasphemare* from the Greek *blaspemein*, which means 'to blaspheme' (see Mirriam-Webster, origin of 'blame'). When you blame others you give them dominion over you, which only God should have. Blaming others therefore is tantamount to blasphemy.

Many of us blame our circumstances and use them as excuses, unaware that we are making them our masters. You say, I can't because:

I am too poor: You empowered poverty and gave it authority to have a grip on your life.

I am black: You empowered racism.

I am from the ghetto: You empowered the ghetto's grip on your life.

I was abused: You empowered abuse.

Blaming your circumstances does nothing but make you a subservient prisoner. The reality is God has always chosen persons in undesirable situations to do His will and to inspire us:

Joseph: from a troubled home; a slave; a prisoner – but became a ruler.

Samuel: was adopted – but became the High Priest.

Deborah: a female in a male-dominated world – became a judge and led Israel to forty years of prosperity.

Moses: under the threat of death from birth; was discarded and abandoned as a baby; was adopted; was a murderer and a fugitive – but became one of the greatest liberators and leaders of all time.

David: was rejected by his brothers – but became a great musician, writer, warrior and king.

Solomon: the product of the adulterous and murderous relationship of David and Bathsheba; was not the first son and therefore not next in line to be king – but still became king.

Jesus: born into humble beginnings; from a town that they said no good thing could come out of – but became the Savior.

Paul: was a persecutor of Christians – but became one of the greatest Christian leaders.

Adam: made from dirt – but became the first man.

Do not let your circumstances define you or confine you. Regardless of your circumstances you have the ability to act: You have the responsibility. If you truly want power over your circumstances then blame yourself. By doing so you don't condemn yourself, you empower yourself. Take all the 'response-ability' for what is going on in your life. The most powerful tool in this situation is confession. Silence is a great way to retain authority, but confession is an even greater tool. Take the blame and empower yourself to make a powerful change in your life. Jesus hung on the cross and took all the blame for all of our sins, empowering Him to break Satan's dominion by taking the blame for Adam's and Eve's sin and by keeping silent. Jesus used this same strategy, as it was prophesied He would, by keeping silent when He was being accused. The key here, though, is false blame. Adam's placing of blame on Eve was false because he was ultimately responsible. Eve's blame on the serpent was false because she chose independently to eat the fruit. The blame placed on Christ was false because He was innocent.

Joseph's actions are a perfect example of what Adam and Eve should have done. He was assaulted and sold into slavery by his brothers yet he kept silent, never casting blame on them. When he was falsely accused of rape and thrown into prison, he again did not make accusations. He ended up more and more empowered in every situation until eventually he was in the seat of power. When you blame your circumstances for your present state it is false blame because you are ultimately responsible. Satan accused men before God all the time, but men were guilty so the blame was accurate and therefore not empowering. Jesus was falsely accused and this was the difference. This was the ultimate key to getting our dominion back.

There is no power without responsibility. When you are responsible you carry the blame. This is the principle that changed the world twice. Michael the archangel challenged Satan on two occasions. The first was at the death of Moses. The second was at the death of Jesus. When Moses died, Michael and Satan were having a dispute over his body but the scripture said that even in this dispute Michael didn't dare accuse, judge or blame Satan: "Yet Michael the archangel, in contending with the devil, when he disputed about the body of Moses, dared not bring against him a reviling accusation, but said, 'The Lord rebuke you!'" (Jude 1:9 NKJV).

Unlike Adam, who accused Eve, and Eve, who accused the serpent, Michael understood this great principle and even in a heated dispute did not accuse Satan. Firstly, this would have empowered Satan and, secondly, he did not have the authority to accuse Satan. Satan had dominion over Earth and therefore had the rights in the dispute. God himself had to intervene and take Moses' body and bury it in a secret place in Moab where Satan, or anyone else, could not find it (Deuteronomy 34:6).

On the second occasion Michael's actions were very different. We find this in Revelation, chapter 12, verses 7-11:

> "And there was war in heaven: Michael and his angels fought against the dragon; and the dragon fought and his angels,
> And prevailed not; neither was their place found any more in heaven.
> And the great dragon was cast out, that old serpent, called the Devil, and Satan, which deceiveth the whole world: he was cast out to Earth, and his angels were cast out with him."
> And I heard a loud voice saying in heaven, Now is come salvation, and strength, and the kingdom of our God, and the power of his Christ: for **the accuser** of our brethren is cast down, which accused them before our God day and night.
> **And they overcame him by the blood of the Lamb**, and by the word of their testimony; and they loved not their lives unto the death." (KJV)

After the death of Jesus, Michael and Satan were at it again. This time there was all-out war; Michael did not hold back. So what gave him the authority to do so this time when previously all he could do was rebuke the devil? It is revealed in verse 11. "They overcame him by the blood of the Lamb." Because Jesus took on the blame of mankind and kept silent even unto death, He took all power and dominion from Satan.

> "He was oppressed and he was afflicted, Yet he opened not His mouth; he was led as a lamb to the slaughter, And as a sheep before its shearers is silent, So he opened not his mouth." (Isaiah 53:7 NKJV)

Through this powerful principle, dominion was restored on behalf of mankind through Christ. Jesus confirmed this after He rose from the dead and spoke to His disciples:

> "And Jesus came and spake unto them, saying, All power is given unto me in heaven and in earth." (Matthew 28:18 KJV)

The Son of Man, Jesus, not only reclaimed dominion for man on Earth but also received dominion as the Son of God in Heaven. And hence, Satan – who would previously go back and forth between Heaven and Earth accusing men to God, as we saw in Job's story – was finally thrown out of Heaven. Many have been taught that Satan was thrown out of Heaven before Adam and Eve were placed in the Garden but that is incorrect. Revelation 12 explains that Satan was thrown out after the death of Jesus.

The Way

So now we understand how the enemy uses distraction to separate you from your purpose. In fact, the word 'distract' means to 'pull in different directions': *distract* – 'drawn apart', from the verb *distrahere*, from *dis* – 'apart' and *trahere* – 'to draw, drag' (Mirriam-Webster).

The spiritual war raging on Earth right now is about stopping mankind from fulfilling purpose. Adam and Eve were placed in the Garden to cultivate it, to guard and protect it and to have dominion. So what did the devil do? He got them kicked out of the Garden, blocking them from fulfilling their purpose. He also took away their dominion completely, ending their ability to fulfill their purpose. He did not go to them and try to get them to lie to God or each other. He didn't try to get Eve to go to a coconut tree and eat fifty coconuts and commit gluttony. Neither did he try to get them to pervert themselves by lying with animals. He went straight after their purpose, to draw them apart from it. The sooner you understand this the more effective you will be in life. Distraction is the quickest route to destruction. Talented people can seem to end up being the most distracted. You might see a talented female singer release multiple hit songs; then she gets distracted and her life goes downhill until they find her lying lifeless in a bathtub.

Again, the enemy's objective is not only to get you to do things traditionally known as 'sin' but also to do 'good'. This is the method especially used to destroy multi-talented people – people who are gifted at many things. We will go into this in detail in a later chapter, offering instruction on how to choose the right gift to nurture and pursue. However, for the purpose of elucidating the topic of distraction, if you want be successful in life you must choose goals based on your vision. This will establish a clear path to your destination: I call it 'the Way'. Your daily mission is to do everything in your power to stay on your way, in the way. This simple principle is the secret to success in anything you do. Anyone who strays from the Way is like a ship off course. You will never get to your desired destination. Along the Way the enemy will tempt you with many distractions. He will even distract you with success. You were born to be a musician but the enemy uses your loving parents, persons you trust, to encourage or force you to be a lawyer or a doctor because they are noble professions and there is more money and security in them. This is similar to the deception of Eve. The serpent, who was wise and whose advice she trusted, advised her. She fell when she saw that the fruit was good to look at, good for food and good for wisdom. Yes, you would look good in society as a doctor and your certificates would look good on your office wall. Certainly, it would be good to feed your family and you would gain considerable knowledge by going this way. But the question you must ask yourself is, "Is this truly the Way? Is this truly my Way?" If it isn't, you will never be fulfilled. You will never find happiness. Never use money as a determining factor regarding the path you should take. Likewise, never use money as a measure of success.

A 2013 Gallup Poll found that 70 percent of Americans absolutely hate their jobs. Besides that shocking poll, look how many seemingly wealthy people there are who appear to have everything in life but their lives are unhappy, miserable and unfulfilled. That is because they chose the fruit that was good to look at, good for food, and good for wisdom. They lost their Way. They are out of place. They are a shark out of water. The shark is mighty and powerful in the water but put it on land and it's powerless. The water is his Way; stay in your Way.

Outside of your Way, you are counterfeit. It is the enemy's mission to make you a counterfeit. Never let society define your Way. Be the king of your jungle. We all know what animal is the king of the jungle: the tiger of course! Society tells us that the lion is the king of the jungle. However lions don't live in jungles. They live on the savannahs. A lion is made to survive on the savannahs, right down to the color of his mane. His color helps to camouflage him among the high grasses so he can hunt effectively. The tiger, the real king of the jungle with his stripes, was made to thrive in the jungle. The lion doesn't listen to us when we call him the king of the jungle. He doesn't let us define his identity. He doesn't let the title go to his head and cause it to get distracted. He sticks to his way.

The Secret to Being Multi-Talented: Casanova!

Your Way defines and requires focus and discipline. Stick to your Way and let nothing distract you. This is the secret to success. Most successful people are known for one thing. Tiger Woods is known for golf; Michael Jordan is known for basketball; Warren Buffet is known for investments; Bill Gates is known for software. The downfall of many promising rising stars is that they try to do too much and become over-stretched; they spread themselves too thin. Even businesses learn to focus on key products or services instead of trying to do everything all at once.

Over time I began to realize that there is only one thing more frustrating than not knowing your talent and that is having too many talents and not knowing which one to pursue. Interestingly enough, I began to notice that there are persons who are multi-talented and known for many things. So I wanted to know their secret. How did they do it? The answer was illusive until I came across the strategy of a very famous man called Casanova.

Casanova was infamous for having large numbers of women fall madly in love with him all at the same time. So, how did he do it? One woman at a time! Casanova would focus all his attention on one woman. He would give her his all, and was willing to sacrifice anything for her. Soon the woman would reward his attention and sacrifice with her undying love. Casanova would begin to carefully ease away and find another woman to repeat the pattern with. Meanwhile, each woman would remain in love with and committed to him eternally.

While I do not condone the practice of womanizing, I can identify some principles that Casanova used that could better serve more noble initiatives. King David, likewise, focused all his attention on each gift individually before moving on to the next, but only after each one had been refined. Each in turn, he became a shepherd, warrior, musician, writer and king.

You can also accomplish many things. Simply apply Casanova's principle of focus… just not his deviant lifestyle!

Distraction Where You Least Expect It

Finally, I must warn you of the most powerful means of distraction. When you find your Way, prepare to be discouraged by those closest to you – your loved ones. Your loved ones will be the ones to most vigorously oppose your Way. There will be mothers against daughters, and husbands against wives, and fathers against sons, as Jesus said:

> "For I am come to set a man at variance against his father, and the daughter against her mother, and the daughter in law against her mother in law. And a man's foes shall be they of his own household." (Matthew 10:35-36 KJV)

Jesus is not condoning family discord but understands how difficult it can be for your loved ones to allow you to do it your Way. This is because your Way is greater than you. Accomplishing your Way requires something greater than normal human capacity.

I was a young police officer working on Paradise Island in the Bahamas and found myself sitting in front of a multi-millionaire who gave me the advice that changed my life. I hope it changes yours. He said for every successful person, product or business that exists, there is someone who had to take a monumental risk to make it happen; a risk that would have made them phenomenally successful or would have completely destroyed them.

Immediately I decided to leave my job and pursue my dreams. My parents seemed devastated. My father was, to me, the wisest man alive. He told me that it was unwise to leave my secure, well-paying government job to go to college, especially when I didn't have the money for college. Your loved ones tear down your dreams for one specific reason: because they love you. Your dream requires risk and the truth is they don't want to see you get hurt. It is their nature to protect you. Muhammad Ali's wife discouraged him from boxing, not because she hated him or did not believe in his ability but because she could not stand to see him get hit in the ring. Michael Jordan's first wife loathed the fact that he had to be away from home for most of the year playing basketball – not because she didn't believe in him but because she loved him and wanted him to be with her. Nelson Mandela's children never wanted him to go on his protracted missions – not because they didn't believe in the end of apartheid but because they loved him.

Your first obstacle to your dreams will be those who love you. Understand this and it will keep you grounded when those who you expect to be your greatest support don't see what you see. Remember, the Way exists initially in your mind. No one else can see it. They don't begin to see the path until you begin to cut out the trail and pave the Way.

The Secrets

- Man's greatest objective is finding his purpose and fulfilling it. Therefore, the enemy's greatest objective is preventing man from finding his purpose and fulfilling it.
- The devil's biggest weapon is distraction.
- There is a difference between a good thing to do and the right thing to do.
- In life there is good and evil but in many instances both of these are the same. Instead you should seek to do right.
- The devil's most effective weapon is the truth, not lies.
- The devil's ultimate goal is not to make you commit sins.
- The enemy is after your identity.
- Reputation is the key element of both trust and deception.
- When you identify your purpose and set out to accomplish it, you will be tested.
- The key to righteousness is not only following the commandments but also being guided by the great command on your life: The will and purpose of God.
- Satan's greatest skill is the art of counterfeiting.
- Counterfeiters do not destroy money, they copy it.
- When you are not living for the purpose for which you were created, you are living a lie. You are a counterfeit.
- If Satan can make you become a counterfeit by inserting counterfeit elements into your life, then he wins.
- Purpose and life are like the inextricable elements of water.
- Test for a counterfeit by a close examination of its authority and identity.
- Responsibility is dominion. To pass on responsibility is to transfer dominion.
- Whatever you blame, you empower!
- Take the responsibility and blame, and empower yourself to make a powerful change in your life.
- There is only one thing more frustrating than not knowing your talent and that is having too many talents and not knowing which one to pursue.
- Some of the greatest objectors to your dream will be your loved ones. Why? Because they love you.
- Find the Way. Find your Way.
- The Way exists initially in your mind. No one else can see it.
- Your daily mission is to do everything in your power to stay on your Way, in the Way.

Chapter 2: What's This Life For?

I See Dead People

In August 1999, a movie was released that became known and is remembered for one line of dialogue: "I see dead people." The movie is called *The Sixth Sense*. It is about a boy who sees and talks to the spirits of dead people who do not know that they are dead. While the movie was based on fiction, I can assure you that this same scenario is being played out every day in real life.

Like the little boy in the movie, I too see dead people. They are all around us. They live in your house; they eat from your kitchen; they sit in your living room and watch your TV – sometimes even when you are not there. They roam your office at work and sit next to you in the pews at church. I can assure you that if you look carefully enough you will realize that you see them too, and you unknowingly interact with them every day.

The greatest tragedy on Earth is not death, nor is it the dead in the graveyard. The greatest tragedy on Earth is the dead who walk among us. I call them 'the walking dead'. So who are the walking dead? They are those who are animated but not inspired. They have life but they are not alive. They are motion without direction. They have a name but no identity.

When Jesus recruited the disciples, one of them told Him that he could not come now because he had to bury his father. Jesus responded, "Let the dead bury their dead." Who are the dead that Jesus spoke of? Can dead people really bury dead people? Likewise, in the Garden of Eden, God told Adam that the day you eat of the Tree of Knowledge of good and evil you will surely die. Despite God's warning, we see that Adam in fact lived for probably hundreds of years after eating the fruit. Solomon said, "The man that wandereth out of the way of understanding shall remain in the congregation of the dead." Who are these dead and what is this death that the wisest man is talking about? Who are these dead that the Father and Son are talking about?

It certainly could not be you or I, or our family members who are being considered. We are all very much alive. We eat. We breathe. We grow. We must be alive. We move. We walk. We talk. We must be alive. We get up every day; we go to school; we go to work. It would be absolutely nonsensical to state that we are not alive.

How could a woman with a master's degree, who goes to her office every day and answers calls and signs papers, not be alive? How could an honest man who gets out of his bed at 5.am every morning, jumps into the driver's seat of a yellow taxi and takes us where we want to go every day, not be alive? How could a pastor who preaches and lays hands on people not be alive? The answer is complex, yet simple. Let's find out.

The Parable that Changed the World – But We Missed It!

> The Parable of the Talents
> For the kingdom of heaven is as a man travelling into a far country, who called his own servants, and delivered unto them his goods.
> And unto one he gave five talents, to another two, and to another one; to every man according to his several ability; and straightway took his journey.
> Then he that had received the five talents went and traded with the same, and made them other five talents.
> And likewise he that had received two, he also gained other two.
> But he that had received one went and digged in the earth, and hid his lord's money.
> After a long time the lord of those servants cometh, and reckoneth with them.
> And so he that had received five talents came and brought other five talents, saying, Lord, thou deliveredst unto me five talents: behold, I have gained beside them five talents more.
> His lord said unto him, Well done, thou good and faithful servant: thou hast been faithful over a few things, I will make thee ruler over many things: enter thou into the joy of thy lord.

> He also that had received two talents came and said, Lord, thou deliveredst unto me two talents: behold, I have gained two other talents beside them.
> His lord said unto him, Well done, good and faithful servant; thou hast been faithful over a few things, I will make thee ruler over many things: enter thou into the joy of thy lord.
> Then he which had received the one talent came and said, Lord, I knew thee that thou art an hard man, reaping where thou hast not sown, and gathering where thou hast not strawed:
> And I was afraid, and went and hid thy talent in the earth: lo, there thou hast that is thine.
> His lord answered and said unto him, **Thou wicked and slothful servant**, thou knewest that I reap where I sowed not, and gather where I have not strawed:
> Thou oughtest therefore to have put my money to the exchangers, and then at my coming I should have received mine own with usury.
> **Take therefore the talent from him, and give it unto him which hath ten talents**.
> For unto every one that hath shall be given, and he shall have abundance: but from him that hath not shall be taken away even that which he hath.
> And **cast ye the unprofitable servant into outer darkness: there shall be weeping and gnashing of teeth.** (Matthew 25:14-30 KJV)

As an avid churchgoer all my life, I heard this parable on a regular basis. The message in the parable was clear: use your talents. I was sure of this. Until one morning at 3.am I awoke to study, as was my custom, and was led to this particular scripture. As I read this scripture, a revelation exploded within me. A revelation that changed my life and the way I looked at life, purpose, religion – everything. This parable became the basis of what I believe.

This revelation was right there before us all the time but we missed it. Even many preachers missed it. The message that Jesus was delivering in this parable was the most important message of them all. Jesus was ushering in a paradigm shift. He was turning things back to the way they were in the beginning – and we missed it.

In the parable above, two of the servants multiplied the talents that were given to them. The third servant buried the talent he was given and returned it to the master in full. This is where it gets interesting. The master began to scold this servant. He called this servant, who returned all his money to him, "wicked and slothful". The servant did not steal his money; he did not take any of it for his personal use. He did not borrow any of it and then put it back. He kept it safe and returned every bit of it to the master. I searched the entire Bible to see where this servant went wrong – every verse, every chapter. I read the entire Torah – all 613 laws. All 248 do's and all 365 don'ts. No sin could be found that he committed.

Another factor I considered was the awesome value of a talent of gold. A talent of gold was a huge fortune and would be considered a fortune even today. A talent of gold is around 75lbs of gold. That is far more gold than you can carry around. It was equivalent to more than 20 years of pay for a regular person at that time and is worth just over a million dollars today. Now think about it. If you gave someone that much money and you came back and they returned every cent, would you consider that person wicked? I decided to search more deeply to unravel this mystery. In doing so, I discovered that there are two main consequences for failing to use your talent:

1. You Lose Your Talent

There is a very common saying that we have all heard at least once: 'use it or lose it'. This statement holds true for your talents. In the parable we see that the master takes the talent from the one who failed to use his talent and gives it to the one who now has ten. In the Luke 19:26 version of the parable, those witnessing the event protested saying that the one he was giving it to already had ten. But the master's response was merciless in both versions of the story:

> "...unto every one that hath shall be given, and he shall have abundance: but from him that hath not shall be taken away even that which he hath".

In life it would seem that the rich get richer and the poor get poorer. This statement is eternally true. This principle comes from Jesus Himself. That person who is on the move doing something with their life seems to stumble upon more and more opportunities as they go. While that person who's life is stagnant seems to be falling apart and losing everything. This principle is actually more practical than you would think. People are attracted to trees that are bearing fruit. Let's say you are a promoter and want to hold a major concert. Would you sign up an unknown performer to headline the event or would you sign up a well-known act that has a following and can draw crowds? The answer is obvious. You would sign up the tree that is bearing fruit. Therefore the talented singer with a myriad of excuses as to why he will not get out there and polish his talent and bring it to the world will lose opportunities. On the other hand, the guy who is out there making it happen will get the failure's opportunities as well. There are so many sloths out there that the person 'making it happen' will be overflowing with opportunities. He will experience the principle of multiplication which is: $5 + 5 = 11$. The more persons that bury their talents, the more opportunities there will be for the 'doers'. This is because God will never leave His missions unmanned. It is up to you to choose whether you will be a doer or a loser.

People complain all the time about how many successful people are out there making millions of dollars with little talent. Well, the truth is those persons decided to get out there and make it happen, so whether they are the best talent or not is irrelevant. They were out there making it happen with the little talent they do have while others were waiting for an opportunity to drop in their laps. If you use the talent that is inside you, you will get more and more and more. If you don't use the talent that is inside you, the little that you have will be taken away.

2. You Go to Hell

For years I have been going around asking persons, pastors and laymen what Jesus did to the servant who did not use the talents he was given in this parable. One hundred percent of the time I get the same answer: He took it from him and gave it to the one with ten who had multiplied his talents. This is true but it is incomplete. The next thing Jesus did was send the wicked and slothful servant to hell:

> "And cast ye the unprofitable servant into outer darkness: there shall be weeping and gnashing of teeth."

When I first read this verse it made no sense to me. Firstly, I could not comprehend the master calling the servant who gave him all his money back 'wicked'. But now the story went on to an even greater extreme. Again this person did not lie, steal, fornicate, murder or do any sin known to man. So how could the master send him to hell? This made absolutely no sense to me.

Paradigm Shift

Then the revelation hit me. Jesus was ushering in something new – a paradigm shift. Just as He had done with many other principles, He was explaining that we are under a new dispensation. He explained that sin no longer took place when you physically carried it out. He explained that under this new dispensation, murder and adultery takes place when you think about doing it. Further, the old law followed the 'eye for an eye' rule of revenge, but Jesus said that under the new law of Love you should turn the other cheek. Likewise, Jesus was ushering in a new standard of sin. In the beginning, under Moses' law, it was about 'thou shalt not'. Because of man's transgression, man had to be given the law to protect us.

But what was this new paradigm? Jesus said: "*The law and the prophets were until John*: since that time the kingdom of God is preached, and every man presseth into it" (Luke 16:16 KJV).

Jesus is saying that the law and prophets had an expiry date. The prophets of the Old Testament prophesied about Jesus' coming, so once He came their purpose was fulfilled. That is not to say that there are not prophets today – there are. The prophets of old had a different mission from the ones of today. The prophet's role back then was to prophesy of His coming while it was John's role to declare Him when He came. After doing so, John expired. Likewise the law had a purpose and an expiry date. The law was about 'thou shalt not'; the Kingdom is about 'thou shalt'. The law was about what you could not do. The Kingdom is about what you can do. Jesus was restoring us to God's original intent. God placed us in the Garden to 'do'. He never intended for us to be governed by any external law. In the Garden there was as little law as possible. In fact there was one law – don't eat of or touch the Tree of Knowledge. Jesus brought back this same format of having as few laws as possible. He brought it back to one law: Love. Love God and love your neighbor.

So what exactly is this new dispensation? Well, it relates to what is sin. From a scholastic standpoint, both the Hebrew (*Chatta*) and Greek (*Hamartia*) words for 'sin' carry the same meaning. According to Strong's Concordance (266), 'sin' in Greek means 'to miss the mark'. What does this mean? What mark is a sinner missing? Well, under the old covenant you missed the mark by failing to live in accordance with the law. The law set the standard and if you failed to meet those standards you missed the mark. If the standard was 'thou shalt not lie' and you told a lie, you missed the mark. Jesus, on the other hand, was changing the standard to which we are held. The new standard is not based on 'thou shalt not'; rather it is based on 'thou shalt'. The new standard is not based on what you should not do; it is based on what you should do. Man was originally placed in the Garden to *do*. That was God's original intent. The original focus of man's existence was purpose not laws. With this parable, Jesus is taking us back to where we began.

Everything was created for a purpose. Purpose is the reason for being. Therefore, if you are not fulfilling your purpose by using those talents that were bestowed on you then you have missed the mark. You are living in sin.

Consider this: A toaster is made to toast. If that toaster is not working, what do you do with it? You fix it or you throw it in the dump. Jesus gave a similar analogy. He found a fig tree not bearing fruit:

> "The next day as they were leaving Bethany, Jesus was hungry. Seeing in the distance a fig tree in leaf, he went to find out if it had any fruit. When he reached it, he found nothing but leaves, because it was not the season for figs." (Mark 11:12-13 NIV)

The astonishing thing about this verse is that the fig tree was not a barren tree – in fact, it was not even fig season – yet the tree was found wanting and was destroyed. Like the fig tree you were born for a purpose. Like the fig tree you are expected to fulfill that purpose. In the version of the fig-tree parable in the book of Luke, the unfruitful tree was thrown into the fire and destroyed. This brings us to the concept of hell in relation to this principle.

What is this Hell that Jesus was Referring to?

There are a few definitions of hell used in the Bible. However, the one that Jesus referred to when talking about hell was Gehenna. This word is translated as 'the Valley of Hennom' – and this place was very real. In fact, you can still visit it today, without dying. Gehenna or 'hell' was the city dump just outside the walls of Jerusalem. It was located in a valley below the city.

This city dump burned continuously to dispose of the garbage within it. The fire never went out and even the bodies of executed criminals were thrown into this dump. It is from the metaphor of Gehenna that we get the concept of hell. The concept that hell is below comes from the fact that Gehenna is below in the valley; it burns continuously as did the unquenchable dump fire; and bad people and junk are discarded there.

You Must Change Your Purpose!

> There were present at that season some who told Him about the Galileans whose blood Pilate had mingled with their sacrifices. And Jesus answered and said to them, "Do you suppose that these Galileans were worse sinners than all *other* Galileans, because they suffered such things? I tell you, no; but unless you repent you will all likewise perish. Or those eighteen on whom the tower in Siloam fell and killed them, do you think that they were worse sinners than all *other* men who dwelt in Jerusalem? I tell you, no; but unless you repent you will all likewise perish." He also spoke this parable: "A certain *man* had a fig tree planted in his vineyard, and he came seeking fruit on it and found none. Then he said to the keeper of his vineyard, 'Look, for three years I have come seeking fruit on this fig tree and find none. Cut it down; why does it use up the ground?' But he answered and said to him, "Sir, let it alone this year also, until I dig around it and fertilize *it.* And if it bears fruit, *well.* But if not, after that you can cut it down." (Luke 13:1-9)

The persons Jesus was referring to above were criminals who were executed by the state. They were considered the worst of the worst. But Jesus said that there are persons who are just as bad as these vile criminals and who will perish just like these evil, sinful men: and these are persons who fail to repent. So what did Jesus mean by 'repent'? From inception I was taught that to repent means 'to turn away from sin'. I was taught that you did it by going up to the altar and repeating a prayer after the pastor. However, it was recently revealed to me that this thinking is acceptable but incomplete. To get a true understanding of what Jesus was saying here, we have to dissect the Greek word used in this scripture. The actual Greek word used was *Metanoeo* (Strongs Concordance 3340): *Meta* means 'change'; *Noeo* means 'thinking/mind/purpose'. *Metanoeo* therefore means 'to change one's mind or purpose'.

So in essence, Jesus was saying that unless you change your purpose and thinking, you will perish just like the worst sinners who have done the most heinous things. Paul made it even clearer when he said in Romans 12:2: "Be transformed by the renewing of your mind." Jesus went on to give an illustration of what He was talking about. He went on to the parable of the fig tree which illustrated that the tree that does not bear fruit will be destroyed. So, what Jesus was saying in these two consecutive but connected parables was that if you do not bear fruit you will perish. The product that is not functioning as it is supposed to is sent to the dump. When your toaster doesn't toast; when your radio doesn't play; when your microwave doesn't heat; when your soda can is empty, you send them to the dump. Likewise when you are failing to function as you should, according the God's specifications for your life, then you, too, go to the dump. Unless you change your life by changing your thinking and purpose you will perish just like the worst of sinners.

The new paradigm is that you should not lie, steal or murder. All of these are wrong. However, under this new dispensation, 'sin' means so much more than we previously understood. Firstly, if you love your neighbor you would not do these things to him. Secondly, it means that if you miss the mark by not using your talents and thereby fulfilling your purpose, you will not see the Kingdom of God. In fact, you will go to hell just like the man in the parable who did not use his talent.

The truth is God is like a loving father. He wants you to prosper and make him proud. He does not want any harm to befall you. That is why he gave you strict laws to protect you when you were a child. Those laws had a purpose and an expiration date. When you matured into an adult he set you free. Free to become all you were meant to be. Free to discover your true identity.

I Don't Know You

Jesus said that many will come before him and say that I have done this or that for You, but He will say, "I do not know you."

> "Not everyone that saith unto me, Lord, Lord, shall enter into the kingdom of heaven; but he that doeth the will of my Father which is in heaven. Many will say to me in that day, Lord, Lord, have we not

> prophesied in thy name? and in thy name have cast out devils? and in thy name done many wonderful works? And then will I profess unto them, I never knew you: depart from me, ye that work iniquity." (Matthew 7:21-23 KJV)

Notice He did not say that those who do not sin will enter. He said only those who do the will of the Father will enter in. Those who follow God's will for their life; the Father's purpose for their life. Everyone else is a worker of iniquity. We will explain what iniquity is in an amazing revelation in Chapter 5.

A great way to determine if God knows you is to determine if you know yourself. If you don't know yourself then God doesn't know you either. He does not know you because you never allowed Him to work with you. He does not know you because you do not look like the person you were intended to be. He sent you to be a businessman but you are a cashier at a fast-food restaurant. He sent you to be a missionary but you are a lawyer. He sent you to be a world-class athlete but you are a butler. All vocations are honorable except the one in which you are out of place.

Imagine that there is a constant war going on between God and the devil. The battlefield is Earth and God's soldiers are man. God has His awesome warriors ready for battle from the day they were born, sent equipped with all the skills they need to carry out their specific roles within the team to win this war. Each man empowered with a given role, job description and position in this great army. Some are swordsmen, some are archers, some are horsemen, some are cooks, some are messengers, some are blacksmiths, some are foot soldiers, and some are generals. Satan, before fighting the physical war fights a mental war. The true battlefield for the Kingdom is in your mind. Satan's strategy is simple and effective. Sun Tzu said that the best way to win a war is to win without fighting. Satan understands this so he simply gets into the minds of God's soldiers and confuses their roles. He makes the swordsmen think they are cooks and the cooks swordsmen; the archers he makes messengers and vice versa; the blacksmiths he makes horsemen and vice versa; the foot soldiers he makes generals and the generals he makes foot soldiers. As a result the army becomes completely dysfunctional and useless. The army shows up for battle with dull, handleless swords carried by men whose main skill is tossing salads. The army shows up malnourished because those acting as cooks are skilled in killing men, not feeding them. Most of the army doesn't show up because they did not get the message from the unskilled messengers. Those who did get the message showed up without weapons because the true blacksmiths were out riding horses. The army will lose because it does not have the cover of skilled archers or the reinforcement of cavalry on horseback. There is complete anarchy due to the lack of leadership because the real generals are among the ranks of the foot soldiers and there are unskilled foot soldiers leading and making the calls.

Can you imagine an Olympic track and field team where the skinny long-distance runners are throwing the shot-put; the heavy shot-put throwers are attempting to run the 5000-meter event; the muscular short-distance runners are running the marathon; and the discus throwers are running the 100m sprint. While this might seem like such an absurdity to even consider, the fact is this scenario is being played out every day in real life. The question you must ask yourself is, "Am I a cook or a swordsman?"

The truth is no vocation is any better than the next. If the general thinks he is better than the foot soldier, let him charge onto the battlefield without them behind him. If the foot soldiers think they are more important, let them charge onto the battlefield without a general to guide them. Every piece has a purpose – each joint supplies (Ephesians 4:16). Some people are meant to be waiters, some are meant to be maids, some are meant to be street sweepers. The question you must ask yourself is, what are you?

Some of you reading this will be saying, "But I'm just a lowly 60-year-old maid. What good am I to this world?" The truth is you may play a more critical role than some of the greatest men you know. There is a touching old story about Ananias, the man who ministered and healed Saul (the Apostle Paul). Ananias was an old man and was near death. He lamented that his life was unaccomplished and without purpose. He felt like a failure. The story says that God Himself ministered to Ananias telling him that his life was critically important and that he carried out his mission well. Ananias did not see what God saw. To him his life was uneventful and he didn't go out and start a big ministry or preach for God or do anything of significance. God reminded him of that one day, somewhere around 34AD, when he changed the world. He did so by ministering to and healing the man who would become the Apostle Paul. Everything that Paul did for the rest of his life, Ananias was a contributor to. So while it might appear to be one simple act on only one day of a long life, it was the day that Ananias was born for. Ananias' sole purpose was to minister to Paul.

You may think that you are just a nanny but you may be nurturing a future president. Miriam was placed in the life of baby Moses to protect and nurture him. This was her purpose. John the Baptist's sole purpose was to identify and announce the Messiah. You may be a teacher at a high school attended by a future scientist who will invent the cure for cancer. You have spent countless extra hours guiding, encouraging and inspiring that child to stay focused. Therefore you, too, invented the cure for cancer. Just as not only the winning players on the team get a championship ring, the entire staff do also. So too will you receive a crown for your contribution to the success of others.

The Most Critical Thing in Life

The most critical thing in life is for you to find out who you are and, by extension, to find your purpose. That thing you were sent here to do. That problem you were sent here to solve. Those gifts and resources you were sent here to manage. Man has a mandate to manage. Stop procrastinating. Stop making excuses. Stop waiting for your season, like the fig tree. Your season started the day you were born. You fought for and received the greatest gift of all: the Spirit of Life. Life is about endless possibilities, not about endless boundaries. Paul said it best in his letter to the Romans:

> "For the law of the Spirit of life in Christ Jesus hath made me free from the law of sin and death." (Romans 8:2 KJV)

You are free this day. Now get up off your couch, get up out of that cubicle, get out from behind that reception desk and go find your dream.

As stated earlier, in 1999 I was a police officer. I met a very wealthy man on Paradise Island in the Bahamas. His name was Jim. Jim was a friendly old Caucasian American man in his early sixties. I ran into him every day for days and we would talk for hours. On the day he was leaving to return to his home in Kansas, he said something that changed my life. He said, "Lincoln, you are not a police officer."

This was the most ridiculous statement I had heard all day. I was standing before him, fully adorned in my police uniform. He then went on to tell me how he once was a very successful Chiropractic Doctor. He said he did it for the money but he wasn't really happy doing it. Then one day he gathered his family and friends together and told them he was leaving the practice and going into the computer business. His family and friends were shocked. Some laughed at and some ridiculed him. How irresponsible they thought it was. Some of them had never even heard of a computer. But Jim was following something from within that he couldn't explain. He followed his dream and soon after he was far more wealthy and successful than his former business could ever have made him. His story was so powerful that it inspired me to leave the police force and go to college to study computer science and business. Not long thereafter I opened my first multimillion-dollar business.

As a police officer I was like a toaster trying to play a CD. I was out of place. Are you in the same situation today? Out of place and at risk of being cursed like the fig tree. If you are, then chances are that you are one of the 'walking dead' that we spoke about in the beginning of this chapter. If you are, then you need to understand one more thing. Death was not made for man. Death was made for animals because they never received the breath of life. Animals die when their spirits leave their bodies. Man dies when he loses his connection to God. You are dead because you have lost the connection. The truth is it is never too late to become who you are. If you are alive there is hope. Moses didn't start his mission until he was 80 years old. Colonel Saunders did not start Kentucky Fried Chicken until he was over 60. If you are ready to learn how to be reconnected, read on.

The Secrets

- The greatest tragedy on Earth is not the dead in the graveyard, it is the dead who walk among us.
- The first rule of talents: use it or lose it.
- The art of multiplication: 5 + 5 = 11.
- God will never leave His missions unmanned.
- The law was about what you could not do. The Kingdom is about what you can do.
- In the Garden there was as little law as possible.

- Jesus brought back the one law: The Law of Love: Love God and love your neighbor.
- Sin means to miss the mark.
- The original focus of man's existence was purpose, not laws.
- Everything was created for a purpose. If you are not fulfilling your purpose then you are missing the mark.
- You must renew your mind; change your thinking; change your purpose.
- When a product doesn't function according to its original purpose we send it to the junk yard. When you do not function according to your original purpose you will suffer the same fate.
- If you are not living according to purpose then you are living in iniquity.
- All vocations are honorable except the one in which you are out of place.
- Some purposes may seem small but they are critical.
- The most critical thing in life is for you to find your purpose.
- Man has a mandate to manage.
- Your season started the day you were born.
- Life is about endless possibilities, not about endless boundaries.

Chapter 3: Where Am I?

He slowly opened his eyes as he awoke from deep, restful slumber. His was a carefree life of comfort. His father's house was one of prosperity and in it he was the favorite son. As the sun beamed through the window and rested on his face, his focus began to become clear. He rolled onto his stomach, bracing his hands beneath him to push himself up. Then suddenly his reality struck him. He was not on a comfortable bed in his father's house. He was on the filthy, cold, hard ground. Then he remembered his situation. He was in prison, falsely accused of rape. His past life of comfort was day by day becoming a distant memory. His name was Joseph and he was the greatest example of one of life's great principles: Grow where you are planted.

Life's greatest and most difficult challenge is understanding who you are and, by extension, why you are. Many people spend their entire lives never finding the answer to life's most important question. Eventually many persons give up trying to answer this question for themselves and instead become what society tells them to be. They don't understand that this is a death sentence. They don't understand that the first step to finding out who you are is much easier than you think. However, if you miss this first step you will miss the answer entirely. The first step to understanding who you are is so easy a baby could do it.

The First Step

To understand the first step you must become like a child again. There is so much to be learned from them. When a baby comes into the world and begins to get settled in, what is the first thing that he begins to notice? His surroundings. Before a baby of any species begins to notice himself, he begins to notice his environment. Before a baby becomes aware of himself he becomes aware of and begins to experiment with his surroundings. It is not until they begin to get comfortable with this first step that babies move to the next phase of their development. It is highlighted by the use of their new favorite word: Mine! This is when they begin to become aware of themselves in relation to the world around them.

Therefore, the first step for anyone who wants to find himself is to look at where you are. Look at where you were placed. In life everything and everyone was placed in its place for a reason. In fact you can get a hint of the purpose of a thing just by where it was placed:

- A bath tub is placed in a bathroom. This gives us an indication of what its purpose is.
- A stove is placed in a kitchen. Therefore you know it has something to do with food preparation.
- A boat is placed in water.

So you see that by observing where a thing is placed you can begin to understand the purpose of the thing. Likewise, if you begin to observe where you were placed, then you can begin to understand your purpose.

Adam was placed directly in the Garden because it was his purpose to work it. Moses was placed in Egypt because it was his purpose to free his people from it. Joseph was placed in Egypt because it was his purpose to pave the way for Moses. Martin Luther was placed in the Church because it was his purpose to take the word to the common man. Mahatma Gandhi was placed in India because it was his purpose to fight discrimination there. Martin Luther King was placed in black America because it was his purpose to end segregation. Abraham Lincoln was placed in the White House because it was his purpose to end slavery.

The Solution

In 2010, an aging police officer named Tim started dating a young teacher named Nicole. He soon found out that for the last few years Nicole had suffered great hardship and tragedy. A few years earlier, before meeting

Tim, Nicole had been madly in love with a man who she considered her soulmate. They had a son together and their lives were fulfilling and blissful. Soon after, Nicole got the devastating news that she was suffering from Lupus, a debilitating and sometimes deadly disease. The disease affected her kidneys and doctors informed her that they were functioning at just 10 percent and she would soon need a transplant or would die. Her blissful life had disintegrated into chaos and darkness. To make matters worse, while trying to come to grips with all of this, Nicole received a call informing her that her soulmate had just died in a motorcycle accident. Nicole was completely devastated. Life was hopeless. What was there left to live for? The only thing keeping her going was her young son; yet she fell into a state of deep depression that lingered on for years.

One day she met Tim, a police officer, who fell madly in love with her. He cared for her and nurtured her with love. He was a refreshing ray of light. Her situation was becoming more and more desperate because they could not find a matching kidney donor for her, yet Nicole's spirit was lifted by Tim's love and support. Notwithstanding her dire medical prognosis, Tim married Nicole and dedicated himself to being with her until the end. They reached out to all of her siblings and other family members to test to see if they would be a match to save her life, but no match could be found. The list of persons in need of a donor was so long that she knew she would be gone before she found one.

One day as Nicole was getting into her car she collapsed and had to be rushed to the hospital. Doctors informed her that her kidneys had failed and that without an immediate transplant she would die. Nicole was devastated but had by now decided to come to terms with her mortality.

"Why can't you just give her my kidney?" Tim asked in desperation as he stood next to Nicole's bed squeezing her hand.

The doctor explained that unless they were family, the chance of them being a match was 1 in 100,000. They decided to give it a try. It turned out that Tim was a perfect match! The solution to all of Nicole's problems had been perfectly placed in her life all along. Tim found purpose and fulfillment in Nicole, and he found someone that truly became flesh of his flesh. Today, Nicole is doing absolutely well and she is again teaching young people at a school in Florida.

The first question on your path to purpose is, 'Where were you placed?' The truth is you were placed exactly where you were meant to be placed and you were placed there exactly when you were meant to be placed there. When you look at your circumstances, things may seem dark but do not be discouraged. Things appear dark because you were placed directly in the middle of a problem: A problem that needs to be solved. A problem that needs you to solve it. You are the solution to a problem and you were placed right where you need to be to solve that problem. The solution and the problem must be placed together in order to solve the problem. Sickness cannot be healed until medicine is placed there to heal it. The patient cannot be healed until a doctor is placed there to heal her. The malfunctioning car cannot be fixed until a mechanic is placed there to fix it.

We are all born carrying within us the solution to a problem. The meaning of the word 'born' reveals this to us. Born is from the Old English word 'beran' which means to 'bear' or to 'carry'. When you are born, you carry with you the solution to a problem that is plaguing your generation. The solution, you, was placed in the midst of the problem to fix it. You not only carry the solution, you are the solution.

I Am Here

So the question is, where are you? It's time to wake up, get up and look around. It is time to understand that your greatness is wrapped up in the fact that you are present on Earth, placed in the place where you were born to become who you were born to be. I have analyzed the words of the Bible's great men when they answered the great call on their lives. Their answers were always the same: 'Here I Am.'

When God called out "Moses, Moses", from the burning bush Moses replied, "Here I Am" (Exodus 3:4). But where was Moses? He was standing in the same wilderness that it was his purpose to bring the Children of Israel to. He was standing in his place. He was standing in his purpose. When God called out "Jacob, Jacob" in Beersheba, Jacob answered, "Here I Am" (Gen 46:2). Jacob was in the place where his forefather Abraham made an oath, planted a grove, called on the Lord and dwelt – the place that was promised to the seed of Abraham through a great nation. Jacob was on his way to Egypt to be reunited with his son Joseph, the new governor of Egypt, who would bring this promise to reality. When God called out "Abraham, Abraham" on Mount Mariah, Abraham responded, "Here I Am" (Gen 22:11). Abraham was in place on the mountain fulfilling his purpose by symbolically sacrificing his only son Isaac. This gesture was symbolic of God's future sacrifice of His only begotten Son. Abraham's seed would inherit the land on which he stood. All of these men were in the place where they were placed, and ready to answer the call.

Interestingly, God called each of their names twice, apparently speaking to their spirit and physical being. They were alive, in place physically and connected spiritually. In contrast, after Adam sinned, God called his name only once and said, "Where are you?" This was a powerful and revealing question because Adam was now in place physically but out of place spiritually.

Embrace the Darkness

Are you in place and ready for your purpose? I can assure you that when you were born, you were. When you were born you were placed in the right place, with the right family, in the right circumstances, equipped with the perfect gifts and skills you need to fulfill your purpose and solve the problems you were placed in. As we learned in Chapter 1, many persons blame their circumstances for their failures in life. They blame poverty, family issues, their job, race and even luck as the reason why their life is in turmoil. What they fail to realize is that the turmoil is not there to hurt; the turmoil is there to help!

Every good thing begins with darkness. Every positive thing begins with the negative. These may be two of the strangest sentences you have ever heard, but they are true in nature and in spirit. The world began in darkness, without form and void. Every day begins in darkness: "And the evening and the morning were the first day" (Genesis 1:5). The wonderful fruit you ate as a snack today started as a seed planted in darkness, in dirt. Mankind was made from dirt. A beautiful and free butterfly begins its quest for freedom in the constraints of a dark cocoon. You began life after nine months of being in a dark womb.

Life's challenges are there to develop your gifts, test your character and give you value. We could easily shorten the turmoil of the butterfly's imprisonment by cutting open his cocoon and setting him free. That would be so caring of us. However, the butterfly would never fly and his life would be short-lived. You see, it is the struggle to free itself from the cocoon that gives the butterfly the strength it needs to fly and to survive. We could easily free a seed from its dirty surroundings in the ground, but it too would not survive.

Likewise, every day we beg God to remove us from our circumstances and deliver us from life's challenges. We pray to be removed from the very thing that is there to make us great. When Moses arrived at the Red Sea with the Children of Israel, he found himself stuck in a cocoon: The Red Sea before him, mountains at both sides and Pharaoh behind. So he did what all religious people are taught to do. He prayed. Not only did he cry out to God but he told his people to sit still and that God would fight their battle for them. God's answer to Moses blew me away and changed my thinking forever. God replied to Moses, "What are you crying out to me for? Don't tell the people to sit and let me do the work. Tell them to get up and get moving. You take your staff and part the sea, then I will help."

> "Moses answered the people, "Do not be afraid. Stand firm and you will see the deliverance the LORD will bring you today. The Egyptians you see today you will never see again. *The Lord will fight for you; you need only to be still.*" Then the Lord said to Moses, "*Why are you crying out to me?* Tell the Israelites to move on. Raise your staff and stretch out your hand over the sea to divide the water so that the Israelites can go through the sea on dry ground." (Exodus 15:13-16 NKJV)

That scripture initially made no sense to me until I saw that Jesus had the same attitude in similar circumstances. Whether it was the disciples bringing a child with devils to Him to be healed, or it was them being amazed by His withering the fig tree, or them crying to Him to save them because the storm was about to sink the boat they were on, their actions always seemed to frustrate Jesus. He would say: "How long will I be with you; you can handle this situation; Oh ye of little faith; If you have faith the size of a mustard seed you can do this and greater."

When David was faced with Goliath he did not get down on his knees to pray. He took action. Do your prayers for deliverance in your closet before you are in the situation so that when the situation comes, you have the faith and power to act. When Jesus, and later His apostles, met a situation on the street they would not break out into long prayers. They would take action and fix the problem: they would say, "Get up and walk" or "Lazarus, come forth." They would do as God told Moses to do at the Red Sea – speak to the situation, take action, fix it and keep moving.

Imagine your kid coming to you and saying, "Mom, I have a situation that I need you to take care of for me. I have an exam in the morning. My finals test. I really need you to help me out of this situation. I need you to take the test for me."

As a loving parent you would take the same stance that God took with Moses. You would say, "Why are you asking me this?" You would tell him to go to his room, pick up his books, study and go take the test himself.

Stop asking God to remove the challenges from your life when you are equipped to do so yourself. Had there been no Goliath there would never have been a King David. Goliath made David valuable and worthy to be king. David had a bad job. He was a shepherd, which was considered the worst job of his day. David's family cursed at him and tried to chase him away from his purpose. Likewise, Joseph's family hated him – so much so, they got rid of him. Joseph had a much worse job than you could possibly have; he was a slave. Then he had a job as a prisoner. What job are you complaining about today? What job are you using as an excuse as to why you cannot fulfill your purpose?

Listen to the stories of successful people. You will hear tales of triumph over challenging circumstances and perseverance over constant failures. You will not hear stories of perfect families and being born into an easy life with everything dropping into their laps. The problems of your life are meant to define you, to crown you, to write your name in the annals of history and in the Lamb's Book of Life. Remember, you are the light of the world. Light is defined and glorified in darkness.

Escape the Darkness: It's Just a Test

Your cocoon is your vehicle to success. Your test is your path to freedom and fulfillment. Before you can become who you were born to be, you will be tested. There is only one road to freedom and it runs through the fire. Whether you pass, or how long you take to pass, is solely up to you. The Bible teaches us that Jesus was led into the wilderness "to be tested" (Matthew 4:1). Jesus passed His test and qualified for His life's purpose in 40 days. Interestingly, the Children of Israel went into this same wilderness to be tested. Unlike Jesus they were a constantly complaining group of people. They complained to God at every opportunity, crying for food and water constantly. The result of them constantly asking to be assisted with their cocoon was that every one of them (the adults) died in the cocoon (the wilderness); they ended up stuck there for 40 years. Jesus, on the other hand, in the same wilderness never cried or complained for food or water. In fact, the devil tried to tempt Him with bread in the wilderness like the Children of Israel, but Jesus did not fall for it.

For those of you who are constantly complaining about your situation instead of getting out there and fixing it, let me make this clear: God hates complainers!

> "Now the people **complained about their hardships** in the hearing of the LORD, and when he heard them his anger was aroused. Then fire from the LORD burned among them and consumed some of the outskirts of the camp." (Numbers 11:1 NKJV)

> "Neither **murmur** ye, as some of them also **murmur**ed, and were destroyed of the destroyer." (1 Corinthians 10:10 KJV)

> "Your carcasses shall fall in this wilderness; and all that were numbered of you, according to your whole number, from twenty years old and upward which have **murmur**ed against me." (Numbers 14:29 NKJV)

The latter scripture quoted above was the fate of the complaining Children of Israel. In Chapter 1, you might recall that I said that there were three instances recorded in the Bible where Satan himself directly tempted man. I explained the temptation Eve and Jesus. The other instance was Job. God

Himself stated how godly and righteous Job was. Satan wanted to prove that Job was not godly and righteous. Again, you will notice that Satan did not come down to Earth to tempt Job to fornicate, commit adultery, lie, steal or kill. These things are of little interest to Satan. Satan's sole mission was to get Job to complain.

> "But now stretch out your hand and strike everything he has, and he will surely curse you to your face."(Job 1:11 NKJV)

As you learned in the previous chapter, when you blame, you sin against yourself. However, when you complain, you sin against God. If you want to be purpose-driven, if you want to live a life fulfilling and pleasing to God, never ever complain about your circumstances. Never complain about where you were placed in life. Get up, get moving and be the change you want to see. Remember, it's just a test.

Joseph had every reason and opportunity to complain. He was hated and betrayed by his family – yet he never complained. He went from being a man of privilege and comfort to being a slave – yet he never complained. He went from being a slave to being the only thing worse than being a slave: a prisoner – yet he never ever complained. Wherever he was placed he got up, brushed himself off and took action. He was made a slave and he became the best slave he could have been and was promoted. He became a prisoner and he became the best prisoner he could have been and was promoted. And eventually he was freed from his cocoon to achieve ultimate success. Joseph never even cried out to God. He just did what God instructed Moses to do: get up, get moving, take action!

Face the Darkness: It's Just Training

Wherever you are in life today is training for tomorrow. If you excel in your training, you will excel in life and will eventually find yourself in the place you always wanted to be. On the other hand, if you fail the training you will find yourself trapped in the wilderness going around in circles for 40 years, never making it into the Promised Land. To get out of the cocoon you must fight and struggle, push, persevere and keep moving. It is this process that strengthens you and prepares you for the future. The Children of Israel had to be constantly helped along and this is why they were too weak to ever leave the cocoon.

David is another perfect example of how excelling in your training leads to your crown. David was given the worst and most frowned-upon job of his day: he was a shepherd. Instead of complaining about having to do this lowly job while his brothers had their glorious jobs in the mighty army, he tended to his job and became a great shepherd. The challenges were great and on occasion he had to fight a lion and a bear to protect the sheep he was entrusted with. Most of us after seeing the lion or bear (whichever came first) would have run straight back to our father and told him that this job was too dangerous: "Father, please don't make me do this!" But not David. He stayed and faced his training. David's dirty job was training for his future. David was to be a mighty warrior. What better training could he have had than to fight lions and bears? David was to be king. He learned to be a leader and caretaker of men by being a leader and caretaker of sheep. Life tested him and he faced the challenge and passed the test.

Likewise Joseph got his leadership training on dirty jobs. He learned his leadership and management skills as a chief slave running the estate of his master. He stayed and faced his training and excelled. Had he escaped and ran away from slavery and gone back to the comfort of his father's house, he would never have become a great governor. Joseph's next training ground was the ultimate dead-end job. He was a prisoner and instead of lamenting and complaining about his situation, he faced it and became a foreman of the prison. As a result of passing his great tests, he erased the darkness in his life and was released from the cocoon into the glorious role of Governor of Egypt.

Moses' wilderness training also involved a dead-end job as a shepherd tending the sheep of his father-in-law, as a fugitive criminal in the middle of the wilderness. He would have to brave the scorching heat and traverse the desert with the sheep to find water and green pastures for them, to understand the terrain and the wildlife of the desert. Just like Joseph, his life of comfort was snatched away from him and replaced with humbling circumstances. For 40 long years he trained in that desert. In the end, he was the only man alive qualified to lead the Children of Israel through that very same desert.

Back to the original question of this chapter: Where are you? Take a minute and contemplate your current situation in life. Take a look at your life with new eyes and renewed vision, powered by the knowledge and understanding you have just received. Where are you? Were the last few years some of the most challenging years of your life? Were you a victim of the great recession? Did you lose your job, your home, your comfort, your security? May I remind you, this is just a test!

I have learned that the greatest way to excel in life is to grow where you are planted. Like Joseph, excel wherever life plants you. If you want to excel, be excellent. The result is that life will promote you to your intended place in life – your purpose, the glorious place in which you were born to be. Never complain about your place in life. Simply strive to be the best at what you do. Be fruitful and multiply. Life's greatest opportunities will come when you least expect it. Life's greatest opportunities come to those who are too busy excelling where they are to ever see it coming. After training comes the fell clutch of opportunity.

David was so busy excelling as a shepherd and being a delivery boy for his dad, that he had no idea that he was about to collide into his gateway to the future – an almost ten-foot gate called Goliath. Moses was so busy going about his business of being a shepherd in the wilderness, that he had no idea that he was about to collide with his opportunity to be a shepherd of men in the wilderness. First he would have to face a formidable force called Pharaoh.

Embrace your training and be ready for opportunity. As the saying goes, success happens when preparation meets opportunity. Many of us fail because we pray to God to remove the preparation phase from our lives and many more of us pray for God to remove the Goliaths from our lives. You were placed where you are for a reason: Face it! Embrace it!

The Secrets

- Grow where you are planted.
- You don't just carry the solution, you are the solution!
- The first step for anyone who wants to find themself is to look at where they are.

- In life, everything and everyone was placed in its place for a reason. In fact, you can get a hint of the purpose of a thing just by where it was placed.
- Things may appear dark because you were placed directly in the middle of a problem: A problem that needs to be solved – a problem that needs you to solve it.
- To understand the first step you must become like a child again.
- If you begin to observe where you were placed then you can begin to understand your purpose.
- Turmoil is not there to hurt; the turmoil is there to help!
- Life's challenges are there to develop your gifts, test your character and give you value.
- Every day we beg God to remove us from our circumstances and deliver us from life's challenges. We pray to be removed from the very thing that is there to make us great.
- Your test is your path to freedom and fulfillment.
- When you blame, you sin against yourself. However, when you complain, you sin against God.
- Wherever you are in life today is training for tomorrow.
- If you want to excel, be excellent.

Chapter 4: Who Am I?

A concerned mother sat with her 'C' average, under-achieving 15-year-old son. He was mediocre in academics and he abhorred any kind of physical work. He was so lazy that he would even pay his friends and siblings to do his chores. Unlike his sibling, he refused to do any work to make extra money. Due to his laziness his hard-working father would often chase him through the house to go and work with the women. His father was a master mechanic and a military man so you can imagine how frustrating the situation was. His mother advised him to take up Home Economics in school to learn how to cook and sew for himself because such a soft and lazy boy would never attract women. He was a hopeless young chap. He faced the same question that we all face at some point in our lives. Who am I? What's this life for? What am I good for? What do I do with my life? What can I do? What is my gift? What is my purpose?

This chapter will be your guide to answering those invaluable questions, particularly the latter. If you answer these questions within your lifetime you will live a life that is satisfying beyond your wildest dreams.

The young man we spoke of above was eventually able to answer those questions. He grew up to be one of the most recognized names and figures in history. Although he was lazy and uninterested when it came to most areas of life, there was that one thing that brought him to life: when he did that one thing, he seemed to have unlimited power and energy. That lazy boy was Michael Jordan and that one thing was basketball.

The Σquation of Life

To understand who you are, you must understand *why* you are. To understand why you are, you must understand what you are. To understand what you are, you must understand why you are the *way* you are: way is design; why is purpose. Therefore, the following is the equation of life that every human being who passes through the Earth must solve:

You = Way x Why
Way = Design
Why = Purpose

Therefore, in order to find life, you must first find the Way and the Why. You must find the design and the purpose for your life. In other words, you are the sum total of your design and your purpose. Your design is your make-up and function. Your purpose is what you were made to do. A great way to find the design of a thing is to simply observe it. A great way to find the purpose of a thing is to study the design of a thing.

Design

Everything on Earth was designed especially for a specific purpose – every human, every plant, every animal, every insect, the dirt, the rocks and the seas. Every creature has a purpose. As I said in the Introduction, man is the only creature that fails to fulfill his purpose. And it is for this simple reason that most men fail to identify their purpose during their lifetime: They simply don't know how. If they could only understand that in the same way that you can analyze the functions or attributes of a physical thing and understand its use, you can also analyze yourself and find your purpose.

If you analyze a television you will observe that it has a screen. This will tell you that the purpose of the television is to be watched. If you analyze a computer, you will see that it has a keyboard and mouse for input and a screen and printer for output. This will tell you that a computer is different from a TV in that you are able to put information into the device and get information out. So by studying the thing, we are able to identify its purpose.

When you analyzed the TV or the computer what you saw were its gift, ability or talent. You saw its function. What you did not see was its purpose. Many persons confuse gifts with purpose. But the truth is that your gift is not your purpose. Gifts are a part of your design. Let me explain. A bee has the gift or talent of flight. Flying is not the bee's purpose. A bee's purpose is to pollenate plants so they can bear fruit. Flight is that tool the bees use to fulfill this purpose. A boat's buoyancy is a part of its design. It is not its purpose. Its purpose is transportation over water. Its ability to float is the talent it uses to accomplish this task. I will further illustrate.

If I place you in front of a broken door that is leaning on a wall next to a doorway and I give you a hammer, nails, screws, and a screw driver, you can easily identify your purpose. You were placed in front of a problem. You were given certain gifts/tools that are perfect for that purpose. Without any further instruction, you know that you were placed there to fix the broken door. It has been said that if you want to know the purpose of a thing, ask the maker. That is true. However, God hardly speaks because whatever He says becomes law and whatever He says happens. Therefore, God rarely speaks. This is why He often asks questions instead of making statements: "Adam, where are you?" instead of "Adam, you are in the bush", which could have bound Adam to the bushes. This is why when Moses asked Him who He was, He said, "I Am That I Am." If shepherd boy David had asked God what he was and God had answered by telling David that he was a shepherd, then David would have been stuck as a shepherd forever. In the beginning God said, "Let there be light" and light became light. Therefore, light will always be light and can never be anything other than light. Likewise, if God had said to David, "You are a king", then David would have immediately become a king, thereby missing the process of growth and struggle necessary to be a good king.

Then there are some who say that if you want to know the purpose of a thing, you should read the manual, which is the Bible. This is also very true. However, the manual tells us about general purpose that is not specific to our personal lives. It does not tell me whether I should be a doctor or a plumber or an actor. This confuses many people because we tell them to read the Bible to find purpose, but some people want to know their purpose beyond going to church every Sunday and being an usher or singing in the choir. Some people's purpose may be secular in nature. Adam's purpose was to till the Garden. Joseph had a God-given purpose that did not include any religion. It was his purpose to manage Egypt. The Maker never told him this and he did not read this in any manual.

The reason it is so difficult for many persons to discover their purpose is because they are sitting waiting for instructions or they simply don't know what to do. So much is left to us to explore and discover about ourselves and our purpose. Self-discovery is one of the great joys of life. In our broken-door scenario, if you take the tools and go outside and start using them to repair your old car, then you have missed the mark. You are in sin. Fixing the old car may be a good thing but it is not the right thing and the tools you were given are not best suited for that task, so you will find life to be a struggle. Can you imagine a bee trying to do the job of a sheepdog or a sheepdog trying to do the job of a bee?

Purpose is Found and Fulfilled by the Efficient Use of Gifts

David was a multi-talented young man. He was a shepherd, he was an amazing musician, a legendary writer whose writings are among the most read in history, and he was a remarkable warrior. He was one of the most gifted men who has ever lived but none of the talents listed above were his purpose. They were gifts that would be used as a vehicle to get him to his purpose, which was to be king. As previously stated, David's sojourn as a shepherd was to train him as a leader, caretaker and warrior. David's musical skills got him into the palace as a musician for Saul. His musical skills literally opened doors for him. His warrior skills gave him recognition, fame and importance. The point is, if someone was advising the young shepherd boy David on his career path they might have said, "You will be the greatest shepherd to ever live. This is your career." Someone noticing his musical talents might have advised him to pursue and stick with music. Someone seeing his warrior skills might have advised him to stick with being a soldier. The mistake that these advisors would have made was to confuse gift with purpose. Had he listened to any of them he would have lived an unfulfilled life. He would have missed the mark. He might have been a successful musician or soldier but he would have been a successful failure.

Therefore, a way to find purpose is through the development of your gifts. If David had not fully developed his warrior skills as a shepherd he would not have been ready for Goliath. If he had not fully developed his musical skills then he would not have been ready for the opportunity to be King Solomon's musician. So while the question of purpose may be illusive, talents on the other hand are more easily identifiable. So the key is to sharpen and hone your talents and in the process purpose will manifest itself. As you develop and utilize your gifts, doors will begin to open. Think about a car and a driver. You are the car and the Spirit is the driver. The driver can turn the wheel all he wants but it is not until the car gets moving that the driver can truly steer it in the right direction.

Your Design Shows the Way

Everyone wants to know the way to go. What should they do? How should they do it? They run to fortune tellers and spiritual guides to tell them what to do. They could save themselves a lot of money on fortune tellers if they would just simply do some introspection and look at their gifts and talents and determine the best use of the combination of the two. By doing this they will find not only a way, but their Way. The design will determine the Way. Every animal has a way. Because of a duck's make-up it fulfills its purpose in a certain way. It has webbed feet for swimming and wings for flying. A pigeon cannot fulfill its purpose in the same way as a duck. Because of an eagle's design it does things in a certain way; a lion and a cheetah do things their own way and fish do things their way. Likewise you have to find your Way. Noah's way was to build a boat to float on the water. Moses' way was to part the water and cross over on dry land. Joshua's way was to cross through the water. Each of these men's missions was to interact with water but each did it in his own way.

Consider this. Tiger Woods is a professional athlete – one of the greatest athletes of all time. But Tiger was not designed to run the 100m dash. Michael Jordan was one of the greatest athletes of all time but he was not designed to be a boxer. Usain Bolt is the fastest man who ever lived but he is not designed to play basketball.

We began this chapter with a story about Michael Jordan. In that story we found that Michael seemed to not be good for or interested in much, but in the end the study of his design would have led him to his correct path in life. Jordan is six feet six inches – taller than the average man. He has huge hands that can hold a basketball as comfortably and securely as many of us hold a baseball. Lastly, he is naturally athletic. With these attributes Michael should have known that baseball was not best suited for him. Because of his athleticism he could have done well at baseball but he would have missed the mark.

As we live our lives we find that we are all naturally inclined towards certain areas. Some of us are great at math; others of us may be inclined towards speaking. Some of us may be gifted at art; others have technical skills. The key is to pursue the development of your gifts and the doors of purpose will be unlocked, revealing your given path. So get out and get moving. The same principle applies if it is your gifted child whose purpose you are trying to figure out. Even if you don't know the child's gifts yet, the key is to try many things and be observant. Their gifts will begin to become obvious. When their gift floats to the surface you must reel it in, nurture and develop it.

I found my gift for music and singing at the tender age of eight. I was a 4th grade student in elementary school in one of the poorest ghettos of Nassau. I decided to try out for the school's choir because all of my friends were doing it. It was the mid 1980s and so the song you had to sing for the audition was 'We Are The World'. It was the number-one song in the world and it was sung by many of the pop stars of the day, with many of them taking turns singing lead: Michael Jackson, Cindi Lauper, Dionne Warwick, Lionel Ritchie, Stevie Wonder, Bruce Springsteen, Kenny Rogers – all of the big stars led a line or two of the song. I had never sung in front of anyone before so when Mr Edward Robinson called me to the piano to sing, I was timid but proud. As he played the introduction I waited for my cue to start. He looked towards me, nodded and said "Go." I immediately burst out into horrible impersonations of each singer. I did my best Stevie Wonder head movements as I sang his part; I screamed as loud as I could to hit Cindy Lauper's high notes; put on my best nasal voice to impersonate Willie Nelson; and grabbed my crotch and bit my lips as I sung Michael Jackson's parts. The room burst into laughter. So did I. I was so proud of myself. This singing thing felt so good! I felt so alive.

After the audition Mr Robinson called the names of those who had passed the audition. Sadly, I was not in that number. Mr Robinson told the chosen ones to meet back at the music room after school to begin rehearsals. After school the more than 30 chosen ones scurried into the music room and sat in three orderly rows. In the center of the middle row sat the one non-chosen one – me. I had found the one thing I loved. The one thing that made me feel better than ice cream. So what if I sounded horrible in the audition? It felt good.

Something inside me woke up when I sang for the first time and that something pushed me to walk back into the music room. Mr Robinson settled everyone in and began to look the group over. He immediately spotted me. "You!" he said, pointing at me. "Did I pick you?" Before I could open my mouth a kid sitting next to me said, "Yes, you picked him." Mr Robinson asked the rest of the choir if I had been selected. Surprisingly they all agreed. It turned out that I wasn't a bad singer; I was just a bad impressionist. I went on to become one of the main lead singers in that choir.

That little choir from the ghetto went on to win multiple song competitions and awards. That little choir from the ghetto got a chance to sing at Sea World and Disney World. Our Orlando performances opened up an opportunity to be the first to represent our country at World Expo 1988 in Sydney Australia. There was one catch – the trip would cost $70,000.

Telling the parents of poor kids from the ghetto to raise $70,000 was no different from telling them to raise $70 million – it was just as impossible. Each kid had to come up with $2,000 when many of their parents probably made no more than $50 per week. It was decided that the parents of each kid would pay $200 per month for 10 months until it was paid off. We were traveling in one year. Many of the parents could not pay and so they began holding fundraising events selling food and pastries. My mother was the best cook in the country and so she led the charge cooking food and baking cakes and pies. A few months in, we realized that you would have to sell 140,000 cakes at 50 cents each to raise the money we needed. In a population of 250,000 this was simply undoable.

Mr Robinson decided to change the trajectory and teach us all a lesson that would change our lives: Your gift will make room for you. We were not cooks and bakers. We were singers! He decided that we would raise the money with our talent – and sing we did. We sang everywhere: To the rich, to the poor, on the streets, in churches, at McDonalds and we held sold-out concerts that were the talk of the town. We were missing classes every day to go around town singing for money – yet we still maintained 'A' averages. In fact, good grades were a requirement to remain in the choir.

We knew that the task was still impossible but it didn't matter; we were having too much fun to notice. In the end we didn't raise the $70,000. Instead we raised $90,000! It was enough to cover all of the students' and chaperons' travel expenses and give them lots and lots of shopping money! We found our talents, we invested in ourselves and we did the impossible.

You become a success in what you invest in. So get out there and start investing in you. Start investing in your purpose. Start investing in the Kingdom of God. Just do it. If you want to be a writer, start writing. Write a blog or write letters to the editor of the newspaper. Just get started and the doors will open. If you want to be a singer, just start singing. Join a choir, post videos of yourself singing on Youtube. The details don't matter in the beginning, only that you get moving.

Press Your Buttons

If someone puts a contraption in your hand, the best way to figure out how it works is to ask them. The next best way is to start pressing its buttons to see what happens. Life is about exploration. It is about exploring your surroundings and exploring yourself. Tiger Woods' father would have never known his son was good at golf if he hadn't explored it. Especially in early life exploration is of utmost importance. The buttons on a thing cause it to react in a certain way. When you push a button on a stove it creates fire. When you press a button on a CD player it plays music. So where are your buttons and how are they pressed?

In our Michael Jordan story we see that Michael as a boy was like the 'walking dead'. He seemed to be lazy, useless and disinterested, but place him on a basketball court and he came to life. You see, his parents were just pressing his play button and trying to get him to react. It didn't work. But when he was plugged into the right power outlet he came alive. His power outlet was basketball.

Are you plugged in? Have you found your power outlet or are you still connected to the wrong place, just going through the motions like the walking dead? It's not too late. It's time to get out of that cubicle, find your power source, plug in, press play and become alive! So again the question is, how do you find your buttons? What are your buttons?

Your buttons are your emotions. Your emotional reactions are the reactions to your buttons being pressed. Look at the word 'e-motion'. It is what moves you. Emotion is from the Latin word '*emovere*'. '*E*' from the variant of '*ex*' which means 'out', and '*movere*' which means 'to move'. Therefore by examining your emotions you can find what makes you move and thus find purpose. As human beings we have many emotions. Many thinkers including Aristotle and Robert Plutchik have come up with varying lists of emotions. All emotions are a guide to your purpose, but for illustrative purposes we will list some of the core emotions:

> Happiness: Whatever makes you happy is the thing that you were born to do; that one thing that you would do even if you were not being paid to do it. Whenever you are doing that thing your happy button is pressed.
> Anger: Whatever makes you angry you were sent here to fight.
> Sadness: Whatever makes you sad you were born to change.

These are three of your emotional buttons. Your buttons are a clear indicator of your purpose. Take Moses for example: seeing a Hebrew being abused by an Egyptian made him so angry that it drove him to kill. Seeing this pushed his button because it was his purpose to free the Children of Israel from the vicious treatment of the Egyptians. When Jesus was informed that His friend Lazarus had died He wept. The interesting thing about this is that Jesus knew that He was about to go and raise Lazarus from the dead yet He wept. Persons observing thought that Jesus was weeping because of His love for Lazerus, however, the truth is that Jesus' emotional button was pressed because death was what He came to this world to change!

When your buttons are pressed, you come alive. You are able to work tirelessly; you have power beyond your regular abilities. Stories have been told of miraculous things happening when buttons are pushed; of impossible feats being accomplished: Of a mother who could lift a 2,000-pound car that fell on her son; a blind and deaf girl named Hellen Keller who earned a bachelor's degree and became a great author; of oppressed people rising up to overthrow dictators; of a man with no legs competing in the Olympic 100m dash. When buttons are pushed oppressive and unjust laws are changed, slaves are freed and change is delivered. When buttons are pushed cures are discovered, bridges are built and walls are torn down. Get out there and find the place you were meant to be, plug in and power up. Find the things that push your buttons and tear down some walls!

Purpose is Not Always Known

For some, their talents are so peculiar that using them to identify purpose is as arduous and illusive as deciphering the Book of Revelation. Think about it; Joseph was an interpreter of dreams. That was his major gift. How could he or his parents have looked at that special skill and identified that he would become a great ruler. There is no correlation. Hence the necessity to apply the previously learned principle: You will find purpose through the development of your gifts. Joseph's gift opened the door for what he was to become – Governor. However a closer look at Joseph's skills would have revealed that he was a governor all along. From his father's house his special gifts drew the envy of his siblings. As a slave he proved to be an exceptional manager and the entire estate was eventually placed in his care. The estate prospered because of his presence. As a prisoner he also proved to be a great leader and was made foreman. He was born to manage. That is what he was – a great manager! But that is the 'what'. 'Why' is the greater question. The truth is Joseph died without ever truly knowing why he existed. After becoming governor he felt like his purpose was to be the governor (Gen 45:8) but the governor was what he was, not why he was. Joseph had a greater purpose that not even he could understand. Joseph's purpose was to set the stage for the great showdown between Pharaoh and Moses.

Moses' purpose was to lead the Exodus of Hebrews from Egypt. This had to be done to fulfill a prophecy made to Abram in Gen 15:13-14. It was the reason he was born – to save the Children of Israel from the land and clutches of Pharaoh. However, there was a major problem with accomplishing this mission and Joseph was born to solve that problem. You see, before Joseph came along Pharaoh did not have a vast kingdom or own the land from which the Children of Israel would be rescued. Pharaoh was a small-time ruler and not a big challenge worthy of God. He was not a king as we know them today. Today we have come to know a king as the one who owns everything in the land – all the money, all the cattle, all the land, and all the people would belong to the king, and he taxes them heavily. Pharaoh and the other rulers of his day were not all-powerful as the kings after them would come to be. They were unquestionably leaders but the land and the people did not belong to them and they did not tax the people. So how could you free a people from bondage if they were not really in bondage? Thus it was Joseph's role to fix this problem by becoming the most powerful person in the land. The most powerful person in the land is not the king but rather the king-maker. Joseph's role was to create the king from whom the Children of Israel would be freed (Genesis 47 KJV):

> "[7] And Joseph brought in Jacob his father, and set him before Pharaoh: and Jacob blessed Pharaoh…
> [13]…And there was no bread in all the land; for the famine was very sore, so that the land of Egypt and all the land of Canaan fainted by reason of the famine.
> [14] And Joseph gathered up all the money that was found in the land of Egypt, and in the land of Canaan, for the corn which they bought: and Joseph brought the money into Pharaoh's house.
> [15] *And when money failed in the land of Egypt, and in the land of Canaan, all the Egyptians came unto Joseph, and said, Give us bread*: for why should we die in thy presence? for the money faileth.
> [16] *And Joseph said, Give your cattle; and I will give you for your cattle, if money fail.*
> [17] *And they brought their cattle unto Joseph: and Joseph gave them bread in exchange for horses, and for the flocks, and for the cattle of the herds, and for the asses: and he fed them with bread for all their cattle for that year.*
> [18] When that year was ended, they came unto him the second year, and said unto him, We will not hide it from my lord, how that our money is spent; my lord also hath our herds of cattle; there is not ought left in the sight of my lord, but our bodies, and our lands:
> [19] *Wherefore shall we die before thine eyes, both we and our land? buy us and our land for bread, and we and our land will be servants unto Pharaoh*: and give us seed, that we may live, and not die, that the land be not desolate.
> [20] *And Joseph bought all the land of Egypt for Pharaoh; for the Egyptians sold every man his field, because the famine prevailed over them: so the land became Pharaoh's.*
> [21] And as for the people, he removed them to cities from one end of the borders of Egypt even to the other end thereof.
> [22] Only the land of the priests bought he not; for the priests had a portion assigned them of Pharaoh, and did eat their portion which Pharaoh gave them: wherefore they sold not their lands.
> [23] Then Joseph said unto the people, Behold, I have bought you this day and your land for Pharaoh: lo, here is seed for you, and ye shall sow the land.

> [24] And it shall come to pass in the increase, that ye shall give the fifth part unto Pharaoh, and four parts shall be your own, for seed of the field, and for your food, and for them of your households, and for food for your little ones.
> [25] And they said, Thou hast saved our lives: let us find grace in the sight of my lord, and we will be Pharaoh's servants.
> [26] *And Joseph made it a law over the land of Egypt unto this day, that Pharaoh should have the fifth part*, except the land of the priests only, which became not Pharaoh's."

Joseph created the model that would later be followed by all future kings. First the king had to be blessed. So Joseph brought Pharaoh before his father Jacob who blessed him. Then Joseph took control of all the money and livestock in the land. Next he took all the land and finally he made all men Pharaoh's servants. Lastly, he taxed them heavily. Pharaoh would become the first of the all-powerful kings.

Joseph had no idea why he was fulfilling the mission that he was. In fact, the person he was paving the way for (Moses) was yet to be born. After Joseph and all his brothers had died a new Pharaoh, who did not know Joseph, emerged. Joseph's descendants had grown tremendously in number and prosperity. The new Pharaoh felt threatened by them and subjugated them to hard labor and vicious treatment. Enter Moses, who was placed directly into the heart of the problem to solve it. Joseph died without ever knowing exactly why he was doing what he was doing. Yet he fulfilled his purpose perfectly, not by knowing his purpose, but by developing and utilizing his gifts to their fullest potential. As you are reading this you may have no idea what your purpose is. Moses never knew his until he was eighty and Joseph died without ever knowing his, but they both fulfilled purpose to the fullest. While purpose is sometimes illusive, gifts are self-evident. Follow your gift; it knows the Way.

The Secrets

- Every creature has a purpose. Man is the only creature that fails to fulfill purpose.
- There is that one thing that brings you to life: that one thing that when you do it, you seem to have unlimited power and energy.
- The Σquation of Life:
- You = Way x Why
- Way = Design
- Why = Purpose
- Therefore in order to find life you must first find the Way and the Why. You must find the design and the purpose for your life.
- Your gift is not your purpose.
- Gifts are a part of your design.
- God hardly speaks because whatever He says becomes law and whatever He says happens.
- Some people's purpose may be secular in nature.
- The reason it is so difficult for many persons to discover their purpose is because they are sitting waiting for instructions.
- Self-discovery is one of the great joys of life.
- Purpose is found and fulfilled by the efficient use of gifts.
- If someone puts a contraption in your hand, the best way to figure out how it works is to ask them. The next best way is to start pressing its buttons to see what happens.
- Life is about exploration. It is about exploring your surroundings and exploring yourself.
- The buttons on a thing cause it to react in a certain way: Push your buttons and see what happens.
- Your buttons are your emotions.
- Your buttons are a clear indicator of your purpose.
- When your buttons are pressed you come alive. You are able to work tirelessly; you have power beyond your regular abilities.
- Purpose is not always known.

Chapter 5: What Is Your Name?

You Can Determine the Identity of a Thing by What it is Called

The name of a thing is extremely significant. Names are so important that many Bible characters have had name changes when they found their purpose. Abraham (formerly Abram), Israel (Jacob), Peter (Simon), and Paul (Saul) are a few who changed their names when they found a new life. The word 'name' has been accepted to mean authority. Authority is your source of right or calling. Hence we can deduce that it is most fitting for a thing to be named based on its purpose or at least its function. Think about it; your occupation is sometimes called your calling. That thing that you were called to do. For example, television means 'vision from afar'. The purpose and function of the device can easily be deduced from its name. A telephone means 'sound from afar'. A car is a breakdown of the old term 'carriage', which is from the term 'horse and carriage'. The original cars were called horseless carriages, later shortened to 'car'. Again, the purpose and function is in the name. Hence a thing is commonly identified by what it does. A toaster toasts; a washing machine washes; a house houses. A chair is from the Old French word *chaiere* which means 'seat'.

You also identify yourself by what you do. You do it every day when you say:

> I am a teacher.
> I am a salesman.
> I am a lawyer.
> I am a bus driver.

By saying "I am a teacher" you are identifying what you are called and what your calling is. It is not much different from saying "I am Joseph" or "I am Mary". Historically many names were based on a person's occupation.

Hence names like Butler, and Smith. The fact is you identify a tree by its fruit not by its leaves or by its trunk (Luke 6:44). If a tree produces oranges, it's an orange tree. If a tree produces coconuts, it's a coconut tree.

What Are You Called?

This sub-topic is not directed at you personally. You know your name and you know what you are called on a day-to-day basis. This one is about us – all of us. When you ask a person, "Who are you?" they would definitely answer you by telling you what they are called. They would reply, "I'm Michael" or "I'm the plumber." You would then attach the name appropriately: "Oh, you're Michael, my sister's friend" or "Oh, you're the plumber. You came to fix the sink."

So who are we? The appropriate answer would be to state what we are called. So, what are we called?

Human
Man
Mankind

Those are three of the many names we call ourselves but what does it mean to be human? Literally, what's in a name? We all know that your name is your calling and authority, but what else is there to a name? What is the real significance of a name?

A thing carries the name of its origin. This is critically important. Remember, name is authority and every authority has to have a source. It must be rooted from somewhere. Every product carries a name which is its source of power and authority. I am typing this book on a Sony laptop. I talk to my friends on a Samsung phone. I have never met Mr Samsung or Mr Sony or Mr Honda, who made my car, but I know them. I know them through their products. People are also branded in this way. You carry the name of your family. In the Bahamas, where I am from, they can tell a lot about you by your family name. They can tell which island you descended from, they can tell your socio-economic status, and they would sometimes even judge your character by it. Just as they can determine your family connections by looking at your features, they can determine a lot from your name.

I Am a Brand

There is a new fashionable statement going around: "I am a brand." In business people are now saying that they are a brand. Up-and-comers are saying that they have to brand themselves. This is so true. You are a brand, but do you understand what a brand is? Every product carries the brand that is the image of the maker, so it can be identified as the maker's product. Brand originally meant to burn an identifying mark (an image) onto something so as to identify ownership. In other words, the thing carries the image of the maker. The image of the maker makes the thing more valuable. The image of the maker makes the thing more valuable than the function and ability of the thing. Would you buy a bottle of juice off the shelf that has no labeling? Would you buy a bottle of pain medicine off the shelf that is not labeled? The brand gives the thing value, good will, and trust. So, yes, through fulfillment of purpose you do become a brand; however, without the brand of the maker you are of little value. The image of the maker gives you authority. Without it you are a brand but a generic brand at best.

But here is the great mystery. The maker also benefits from the brand of the product. Consider this, without the Mac computer or the iPhone what would Apple be as a company? Who would know of them? They would be completely unknown. Movie studios understand this principle, so when they advertise a new movie they say, "From the producers of the previous hit movie…" Booksellers do the same when they say, "Author of #1 bestseller…"

The maker is known by its product. Hence it is fair to say the maker gets the glory from the brand. Are you truly a brand or are you a generic product? You truly become a brand when you conform to the design of and do what it is your maker intended. The product must work according to the specifications of the maker otherwise it is of no value. If a car doesn't work properly it is recalled. If it does work properly it is glorified by the maker. We see this principle in use when God says, "I am the God of Abraham, Jacob and Isaac." God is making Himself known through his product. Is

God able to make Himself known through you? Are you living according to your design and specifications?

The first thing God gave to man was His image and likeness. The image is his brand. The likeness is similitude. So what is the deeper meaning of likeness? A product is designed by the maker. The maker is defined by the product. A computer company makes computers. So if you are looking at a computer then you know its maker is a computer company. Additionally, each computer made by the company is made with similar specifications. They may have different physical attributes – different colors, etc. – but they are made 'like' the maker envisioned them to be made. In Genesis 1:26, God said: "Let us make man in our image and according to our likeness." The key word there is 'according'. So it means 'based on our specifications or standard'. So likeness is more than just looking like the maker. In fact, we don't physically look like God at all. God is spirit; He is of the unseen so He doesn't have a physical look. All of Henry Ford's cars are made with his image and likeness but the cars don't resemble Henry Ford. They carry his brand, design and specification. We will break this concept down further in the next chapter.

The Name

Now that we have a deeper understanding of names we can go back to our question: What are we called? With our new understanding, we know that the thing gets its name from the maker. Just like you got your name from your family and a product gets its name from its maker. So what is the name of our maker? He is called many things but what is His name? Our Maker is called names like:

God
Father
Yahweh: YHWH
Jehovah
Jah
Adonai
El-Shaddai
Elohim

All of the above are used to refer to God. If you used any of these names, persons would generally know to Whom you are referring. But the truth is, none of the above are God's name. Shocking, I know. All of the above are actually titles, *not* His name:

God is a title: It is What He Is and What He does.
Father is another title: Again, it is What He Is and What He does.
Yahweh or YHWH is not His name, it is His title: It simply means 'Lord'.
Adonai also means 'Lord': It is Jewish custom to revere and therefore not call the name YHWH, therefore they use the term Adonai instead.
Jehovah and Jah are also titles: They also mean 'Lord'.
Elohim means 'God'. It, too, is a title.
El-Shaddai means 'God Almighty'.

I realize this is confusing. We have basically gone through all of the names that we commonly use to refer to God, yet we find that not one of them is His name. What we have is something similar to students calling someone teacher. Whenever they call to them they say 'teacher, teacher'. Teacher is not his name but it is what they call him. You call your mother 'Mom' or 'Mommy'. You never ever refer to her name unless you are identifying her to a stranger. Yet Mom is not her name. It is what you call her. It is what she is but it is not her name. So we are still left with the problem, how do we find our name if we don't know the name of our Maker?

This issue was problematic for the Israelites of old also, so much so that they simply called Him 'Hashem'. Translated, it means 'The Name'. The title YHWH was revered by the Israelites, so out of respect they did not use it. This left them without a name for everyday use. So they called Him Hashem. This is where Jewish people get the name 'Semite' from, or Semitic people; they are literally people of 'The Name'.

This led to another problem; eventually, mankind began to forget about God. Moses' first conversation with God is evidence of this. Moses did not know who God was and he didn't know if the Children of Israel would know who God was. This was when God revealed His true name and Identity (Exodus 3:13-15):

"And Moses said unto God, Behold, when I come unto the children of Israel, and shall say unto them, The God of your fathers hath sent me

unto you; and they shall say to me, What is his name? what shall I say unto them?
And God said unto Moses, **I Am That I Am**: and he said, Thus shalt thou say unto the children of Israel, **I Am** hath sent me unto you.
And God said moreover unto Moses, Thus shalt thou say unto the children of Israel, the Lord God of your fathers, the God of Abraham, the God of Isaac, and the God of Jacob, hath sent me unto you: **this is my name for ever, and this is my memorial unto all generations."** (KJV)

This is a wonderful revelation. God's name is and shall forever be 'I AM'. That's His name – simple and powerful. Now the question is, how is that related to us?

Our Name

So we have come to the conclusion that the thing gets its name from the maker. The truth is we call ourselves by this name every day. Likewise people call us by this name every day. Every time you say "I am Charles Smith" you have identified yourself by God's name. You know your name as Charles Smith. This identifies your family name and your personal name. When you say "I am Charles Smith" you are also identifying your family connection to and carrying the name of God. 'I am' is more than a pronoun and a verb; it is your family name.

Let me prove it. What was the name of the first man? If you said Adam, you are correct. Adam carried all of mankind inside him. He is our earthly father and therefore we carry his name. Here's the proof (Genesis 5:2):

"Male and female created he *them*; and blessed *them*, and called ***their* name Adam**, in the day when they were created."

This is amazing! So God called us Adam – all of us! We carry the name of our father Adam and thus we are all Adams! This revelation is most powerful when you understand the meaning of the word 'Adam'.

So, Who Are We?

What I am about to reveal to you is the most powerful revelation of them all. It is the true and powerful Gospel. It is the reason that Christ came and died. It is the understanding of the Kingdom of God. It is God's original intent. It is the reason you live and breathe. It is the reason you were created. Understand what I am about to say to you and you will live abundantly. You will never taste death and you will find true comfort, pleasure and fulfillment in this life. Most importantly you will understand who you are.

If you look at the Hebrew word for 'man' you will find something interesting. The Hebrew word for 'man' is *Adam* (Strongs 120). There is much mystery that can be revealed in words. Break down the word 'Adam' and you will see it. Ad-AM. I like to say Adam is the 'Addition to AM'. Man is the addition to God. We get our name directly from God.

Now let's take a deeper look. What does 'I Am' actually mean in the original context? The Hebrew word for 'I AM' is *Hayah* (Strongs 1961). *Hayah* means to 'be' or more directly to 'become'. So if God says 'I Am Who I Am', it means I become who I become. The words 'be' and 'is' carry the same context. What you *be* is what you *are*. The Hebrew word for 'man' (singular instead of mankind) is *ish*. So, for example, if you say that someone is Jewish, you are saying that they are a 'Jew Man'. If you call yourself Jewish you are also saying that a Jew is 'what I be'. The word *ish* is derived from the word 'is'. I hope this revelation is beginning to take root in your heart.

But wait, there's more. Let me give you another phonetic example to illustrate my point. 'To be' means 'to exist'. Let's break down the word 'ex-ist'. 'Ex' means 'to make' or 'become' (for instance, extend means 'to make or become long': 'ex' means 'make'; 'tend' means 'long'), and 'ist' means 'man'. So, 'to exist' means 'to become man'. 'Ist' has to do with your essence, what you are, what you are about. Therefore, if you say a man is racist then he is about race. If you say a man is a physicist then he is about physics. You can also say that he is a physics man. Mirriam-Webster says that the word 'exist' is from the Latin word *existere*. It says *ex* means 'to come' and *istere* means literally 'to stand', but the actual meaning is 'being'. So 'to exist' means 'to come into being'. Man is sometimes referred to as 'beings'.

So God called himself 'I AM' which means 'I be'. Man is 'ish' which also means 'to be'. But what does this mean? What is the significance of us being called the same thing that God is called? Is it merely, as we explained earlier, a matter of branding? Is it merely about the fact that you carry the name of your Father, or is there some greater significance? I put it to you that it is of the greatest significance of existence. There is nothing more important. There is nothing more critical.

Who We Truly Are

We call ourselves many things: Human, human beings, Christians, Muslims, Buddhists and so on. Certainly we have so many titles. Many of these titles describe who we are but none of them truly define who we are. Human is a compound word, it means: 'Hu' – dust or dirt (literally 'red dust'); and 'Man' – meaning 'man'. So it is a term that describes that we were made from the dust. We will explain the significance of all of these earthly titles more in the next chapter. The truth is we give ourselves these titles in an effort to understand who we truly are. Hard as we try, the only conclusions we come to are descriptions of our selves. Who we truly are still remains a great mystery to most people. This entire book thus far, and especially this entire chapter, has been leading to the revelation of this one great mystery. The true Gospel of Christ! The true Gospel of the Kingdom! The true Gospel that sets you free!

> "*For those who are led by the Spirit of God* ***are the children of God***. The Spirit you received does not make you slaves (servants), so that you live in fear again; rather, the Spirit you received brought about your adoption to **Sonship**. And by him we cry, Abba, Father." The Spirit Himself testifies with your spirit that we are **God's children**. Now if we are children then we are heirs – Heirs of God and co-Heirs with Christ..." (Romans 8:14-17 NKJV)

This is one of the most powerful and important scriptures in the Bible. If you had read no other scripture in the Bible, this scripture alone would have been enough for you to understand everything. All of life's questions can be answered in this one scripture. It tells us who we are and where we are from.

Read deeper and you will see that it also reveals what we can do and where we are going. But the point of this section is to reveal who we are.

The scripture tells us we are sons of God. Yes, you have heard it before but what does that mean? To call yourself a son of God is more important than calling yourself a Christian. To call yourself a son of God is even more important than calling yourself a human being. Why?

> If a dog has a son what is it? A dog.
> If a cat has a son what is it? A cat.
> If a lion has a son what is it? A lion.
> So if God has a son what is it? A god.

In Exodus 7:1 (KJV), God said to Moses, "See, I have made thee *a* god to Pharaoh." David stated in Psalms 82:6 (NKJV): "I said, You *are* gods, And all of you *are* children of the Most High."

If you don't want to take David's word for it then take the words of Jesus. He quoted David when the Jews wanted to stone him for saying the same thing (John 10: 33-38 NKJV):

> "The Jews answered Him, saying, 'For a good work we do not stone You, but for blasphemy, and because You, being a Man, make Yourself God.' Jesus answered them, 'Is it not written in your law, "I said, You are gods"?' If He called them gods, to whom the word of God came (and the Scripture cannot be broken), do you say of Him whom the Father sanctified and sent into the world, 'You are blaspheming,' because I said, 'I am the Son of God'? If I do not do the works of My Father, do not believe Me; but if I do, though you do not believe Me, believe the works, that you may know and believe that the Father *is* in Me, and I in Him."

This is an amazing and revealing scripture. This is what Jesus has been trying to tell us all along. We are sons of God. We are co-heirs with Christ. Do you understand what it means to be a co-heir with Christ? It means that He is your brother and you share entitlements with Him. We are no longer servants but sons. God never intended for us to be His servants. He created sons, not servants:

> "And because ye are sons, God hath sent forth the Spirit of his Son into your hearts, crying, Abba, **Father**. Wherefore thou art no more a servant, but a son; and if a son, then an heir of God through Christ." (Galatians 4:6-7 KJV)

From this day forth you will realize and understand that you are not a servant but rather a son of God. You are the son of the Great and wonderful I Am. From this day forth you will understand that when you say "I Am" it is more than a declaration. It is a birthright! It is who you are and it is Whom you are from. This is what the scripture means when it says, "Thou shalt not take the Lord's name in vain." Many have misunderstood this as saying that it means don't say the Lord's name. Notice it does not say, "Thou shalt not say the Lord's name in vain." It says, "Though shalt not take the Lord's name in vain." The word used is 'take', which in Hebrew is *Nasa* or *Nasah* (Strongs 5375). This word is used 653 times in the Bible. In none of those instances is it referring to speaking or saying. *Nasah* means: *to take, lift, carry*, or *to bear.* What God commanded is that you should not carry His name in vain; to not bear His name in vain. When you say "I Am" you are carrying the name of the Most High God. When you say "I Am" you are carrying or bearing the name of your Father. When you say "I Am" you are bearing your family name. When you say "I Am" it must not be in vain – it must have meaning. When you say "I Am" it must have purpose. When you say "I Am" you are tapping into the great and powerful connection.

God could have given Himself any name He wanted. The fact is He is God; He can do as He pleases. He chose the name I Am for one specific reason. It is the same reason that the Bible says that God cannot lie. As I said earlier, God hardly speaks because whatever He says becomes, and whatever He says becomes law. God cannot lie because whatever He says becomes the truth. So God has to be extremely careful about what He says. Therefore, no other name would do. I once asked Dr Myles Munroe why he did not call himself Rev Myles or Rev Dr Myles. He replied that you should never let people classify you, because if they can classify you then they can cancel you out! He said that Dr Myles can appeal to colleges, corporations, governments or churches. Rev Myles is classified as a Christian, so only Christians will listen to him.

Likewise God does not want to be classified and therefore God's name is that 'He is'; His name is that 'He becomes'. Whatever He needs or wants to be, He becomes. Whether you know it or not, you have this same wonderful problem! Whatever you say, you become. That is why you should never speak negative words about yourself. You should never say "I am a failure" or "I am ugly" or "I am not happy." Instead you should use the power and authority of your 'I Am' family name to speak life:

> I am Saved!
> I am Redeemed!
> I am Delivered!
> I am Healed!
> I am Successful!
> I am Important!
> I am Beautiful
> I am that I am, that I am!

The statement 'I Am' is so powerful that it is the only time you can lie and still be telling the truth. You can use those powerful words to cause yourself to become what you are not yet. You don't have to wait until you are a success to say "I am a success." Joel 3:10 says: "Let the weak say I am strong!" Romans 4:17 says: "...calleth those things which be not as though they were".

So, speak life to your life today! Use the power of your family name to become who you were born to be. To become who you are. To become who you AM! If you were born to be a leader, say it! I Am a Leader. If you want to be a success, say it! I Am a Success. Do not say I will be a success. There is little power in that statement. But there is power and authority in the mighty name of God. I Am a Success! Try it! Sometimes it may not make sense. Sometimes it may not make sense grammatically, but it will make sense in the end. It didn't even make sense when Jesus used it (John 8:58 KJV): "Jesus said unto them, Verily, verily, I say unto you, Before Abraham was, **I am**." Jesus' use of the words 'I am' in that sentence made no sense grammatically. His point, though, was not grammar; He was invoking the power of his family name. Christ and you are co-heirs to that name and its power.

'I Am' is so powerful that it forms the words that God used to create the world. The words 'Let there be' that God used when He created everything have the same meaning as 'I Am'. It is the Hebrew word *Hayah* (Strongs 1961). 'I am' means 'I become'. To say 'let there be' is to tell something else to become. 'I am' is personal – it is to speak life, power and existence to yourself.

'Let there be' is the exact same statement spoken to your environment and those in it. So when you say "I am a failure" you are also saying 'let there be' failure. You have the power today to speak life to your environment; to speak life to your situation; to speak life to those around you; and to speak life to yourself by calling on that great and powerful name. Call on His name today and become who you were born to be. Become who you Am!

The Secrets

- You can determine the identity of a thing by what it is called.
- You are identified by what you do.
- A thing carries the name of its origin.
- Every product carries the maker's brand.
- The image of the maker makes the thing more valuable than the function and ability of the thing.
- Through fulfillment of purpose you become a brand; however, without the brand of the maker you are of little value.
- The maker also benefits from the brand of the product.
- To call yourself a son of God is more important than calling yourself a Christian.
- Whatever you say, you become.
- The statement 'I Am' is so powerful that it is the only time you can lie and still be telling the truth.
- 'I Am' is so powerful that it forms the words that God used to create the entire universe.

Chapter 6: The Secret in the Mirror

A weathered old woman stood motionless in the center of her bedroom gazing into the dusty mirror. It was attached to the dresser drawer and, like the woman, was old and had clearly seen better days. The woman frowned as she stared at her reflecton. She appeared confused. I stood in the doorway, also confused, wondering what was going through her head. Gradually, her facial expression relaxed into a blank stare – as if she had given up on whatever it was she was attempting to work out in her mind.

"What are you looking at, Mammy?" I asked gently from the doorway.

'Mammy' is what we called our grandmother. Her answer was devastating.

"I don't know," she said as she turned towards me. "Who are you? Get out of here! Get!"

"It's me, your grandson," I replied cautiously.

"I don't know you! I said get out!" she screamed at me.

I was terrified. I quickly pulled the door shut and went to the other side of the house. She was suffering from dementia – a terrible disease of the mind, similar to amnesia.

Identity Crisis

As I studied the history of man and their struggles, and issues from the Garden up until now, it reminded me so much of the symptoms of my grandmother's dementia. Due to mental illness she could not remember who she was, nor could she remember who I was. She could see herself in the mirror but was helpless to identify who stood before her. She could see me but even though I was her kin, she did not know me and therefore reacted adversely towards me. I have come to the conclusion that mankind's crisis is not a crisis of war or racism or hate or crime or terrorism or pollution. These are all just symptoms of a greater root problem. Man's crisis is an identity crisis.

Man has forgotten who he is, both personally and collectively. Because man doesn't know who he is, the result is that he abuses himself and those around him. Racism stems from the fact that we don't know who we truly are so we identify ourselves by our physical attributes. Like my grandmother, we can identify our skin and our clothes but we don't understand our true essence, which we lost in the Garden when Adam ate the fruit and lost connection to God. If we could come to know who we truly are then we would realize that identifying a man by the color of his eyes, hair or skin is a worthless and futile exercise. It is like identifying cars by their color instead of their make and model. When Adam ate the fruit of the Tree of Knowledge he lost his spiritual vision and his physical eyes were opened. This is why immediately Adam and Eve began to see their nakedness. When you are looking with spiritual eyes, physical appearance and attributes mean little to you. You are able to see through the outer skin directly into the soul and source of man.

Not only is man's identity crisis leading to social ills, it is also leading to personal dysfunction. As stated earlier, the great tragedy is that people are walking around confused and out of place because they do not know their true identity. There is a great singer trapped in the body of a cook. There is a great musician trapped in the body of a medical doctor, and a great actor waiting tables. All callings are acceptable except for the ones you were not called to do.

The Mirror

What I am about to reveal to you is one of the greatest and most powerful secrets known to man. If you are able to understand this mystery, then you will discover and repossess what Adam lost. You will find the Way that leads to the Straight Gate. You will drink from a river of living water and never thirst again. You will eat the bread of life and hunger no more. Your spiritual eyes and ears shall be reopened and you will see the Great Shepherd and know His voice. You will awaken from your slumber and find peace and pleasure in living your purpose.

So, if mankind's problem is that he is suffering from an identity crisis then the first step to solving this problem is to understand what identity means. Ask this question to a million people and more often than not you will get the answer that it is who you are or who you are identified as. Some will say it is your name. But to get the true meaning of a word sometimes requires the need to carry out a little etymological research. That means, let's break down the original use of the word.

Identity is from the Latin word *idem* which means 'same'. The word evolved into the late-Latin word *identitas* which means 'quality of being identical'. So the word 'identity' has less to do with determining who you are and more to do with determining who you are like: hence the link to identical. One of the Merriam-Webster Dictionary's definitions of 'identity' is: 'sameness in all that constitutes the objective reality of a thing: oneness'. Therefore, man's identity crisis comes about not because he doesn't know who he is but because he does know who he is like.

As we learned in the previous chapter, we are sons of God and therefore, as Jesus said, we are gods. However, the mystery is much deeper than that. God made us in His image and in His likeness. This is the base and essence of our identity. But what does that really mean? It means that we are the reflection of God in this realm. We are the mirror image of God. Think about how a mirror works. Metaphorically speaking, a mirror has two sides – the side in which the image lives and the side in which you are. The glass is the barrier that separates (and connects) the two sides. The side in which the image lives is the spiritual realm. The side in which you live is the physical realm. Both sides of the mirror are perfectly synced. They both look exactly the same and they both work in complete unison. Whatever happens in one happens in the other. So if you lift your hand, the image lifts its hand. If you smile, the image smiles. If you frown, then the image frowns. This is the mystery of the Kingdom of God and how it works. You see, the truth is that the image is not the image; you are the image! Our identity is predicated upon our ability to be like God. Without it, we have no identity. Therein is the source of our Identity Crisis, personally and collectively.

Mirror, Mirror

"...as He is, so are we in this world."
1 John 4:17

We are the image and likeness of God. We are the reflection of Him, and Earth is a reflection of Heaven. The first duty of the image is to do the will of the other side:

> "But be doers of the word, and not hearers only, deceiving yourselves. For if anyone is a hearer of the word and not a doer, he is like a man observing his natural face in a mirror; for he observes himself, goes away, and immediately *forgets what kind of man* he was." (James 1:22-24 NKJV)

This scripture uses the mirror to explain this great mystery. You are the reflection of God. The reflection does not do its own thing; it does the will of the other side. When you fail to do the will of the other side, you are like a person suffering from dementia or amnesia and you forget what you are. When looking into a mirror, your eyes are on the spiritual realm not the physical realm around you. You are locked in and in sync. You can see the physical realm but you see it through the mirror as a reflection of the spiritual realm. When Adam sinned, the mirror was broken. Adam turned away from the mirror and looked at himself in the physical realm for the first time. He was no longer in sync with or connected to the spiritual realm. He was no longer doing the will of the spiritual realm.

To fix the problem, God had to become physical and enter the physical realm and become the mirror. He did this through Christ. Like a mirror, Christ is the mediator between man and God. Additionally, Christ came to be our example; to be the mirror that we should follow; to open our spiritual eyes again so that we can see our true selves as the sons and glory of God. He said, "I am the way." He implored us to follow Him and do as He does. He is the gate and, like a mirror, He became the gateway back into the spiritual realm to reconnect us to the other side:

> "But we all, with unveiled face, beholding as in a mirror the glory of the Lord, are being transformed into the same image from glory to glory, just as by the Spirit of the Lord." (2 Corinthians 3:18 NKJV)

Paul makes it perfectly clear in this scripture metaphorically. The mirror image is God in all His glory. You are the same image on this side of the mirror and you are therefore God's glory on this side. Jesus further illustrates this in the Lord's Prayer when He says, "Thy kingdom come, thy will be done, on earth as it is in heaven" (Matthew 6:10 KJV). He was teaching us the mystery of how the Kingdom works. Earth is intended to be a reflection of Heaven. God illustrated this when He told Moses to replicate Heaven on Earth when he built the tabernacle:

"[5] They serve at a sanctuary that is a copy and shadow of what is in heaven. This is why Moses was warned when he was about to build the tabernacle: 'See to it that you make everything according to the pattern shown you on the mountain.'"(Hebrews 8:5 NIV)

The building of the temple was symbolic of the principle of the mirror – that Earth should be a reflection, a mirror image of Heaven.

This brings us to God's original intent, which was to extend the Kingdom of Heaven to Earth through mankind. If you would recall the two key scriptures I referenced in the previous chapter that showed that we are sons of God, they both had qualifications for becoming sons of God. Firstly, in Romans 8:14, it says: "***For those who are led by the Spirit of God are the children of God.***" The first part of this sentence clearly qualifies who the sons of God are: those who do the will of God. Therefore, if you are not doing the will of God then you are not qualified to call yourself a son of God. Jesus demonstrated this while He was preaching and was informed that His mother and brothers were outside to see Him. He told the messenger that His mother and brothers were those who do the will of the Father (Matthew 12:46-50). Jesus also held Himself to this standard:

> "If I do not the works of my Father, believe me not. But if I do, though ye believe not me, believe the works: that ye may know, and believe, that the Father is in me, and I in him." (John 10:37-38 KJV)

You will recall that Jesus was being threatened with stoning for stating that He was the Son of God. But He used scripture to illustrate that we are all sons of God. He qualified it, though, by stating that you can judge sonship by whether one is doing the works of the Father. Then you know that the "Father is in me and I in him"; that the principle of the mirror is in full effect. Jesus further illustrated this in John 14 when He said, in verse 9, that when you see the Father you see the Son. In verse 10 He says that the works that you see Him doing are actually being done by the Father. Jesus went on to reveal that this same principle, and the power that comes with it, applies to us as well. He says, "He who believes in me, the works that I do he will do also." He went on to declare that we will do even greater things because He was going back to the Father on the other side. This is so that the mirror principle can be reapplied to our lives. So now He is back with His Father on the other side and we are on this side carrying out His will.

Now, here is the most powerful and amazing part of the principle of the mirror. It is revealed in verse 13 of the same chapter. The secret is that the mirror works both ways! When both sides of the mirror are in sync not only can Heaven move Earth, but Earth can move Heaven! "And whatever you ask in My name, that I will do, that the Father may be glorified in the Son. If you ask anything in My name, I will do *it*" (John 14:13-14 NKJV). Halleluiah! Do you know how powerful that is? Do you understand that this puts the power of Heaven in your hands? Jesus said:

> "Blessed are you, Simon Bar-Jonah, for **flesh and blood has not revealed *this* to you**, but My Father who is in heaven. And I also say to you that you are Peter, and on this rock I will build My church, and the gates of Hades shall not prevail against it. And I will give you the keys of the kingdom of heaven, and **whatever you bind on earth will be bound in heaven, and whatever you loose on earth will be loosed in heaven.**" (Matthew 16:18-19 NKJV)

Jesus was again explaining the principle of the mirror and how the Kingdom works here. He was explaining that you are to be connected to and can receive your word directly from the Father in Heaven: metaphorically, from the other side of the mirror, not from the physical realm. He further explained that this was the system that He was establishing. His church: the Kingdom of God. When Jesus spoke of the church here He was not talking about a building where we go to worship on Sundays. He was giving them an example that they understood. They were in the Roman Empire and they understood how that system worked, so He was using it to illustrate His point. The church was actually a part of the Roman government. It was the Ecclesia or the assembly/gathering. It was the assembly of the emperor's council. They would receive his instructions and go out into the world and carry out his bidding. Members of the council had powers to be magistrates and therefore could loose and bind persons. This is how the Kingdom of God works. We are His church, which He gathers together daily. He instructs us and we are to carry out His will. These councils, though, also had power to influence the emperor. The scripture above was not directed at Peter. It was to all of us, as Jesus reiterated in Chapter 18:

> "Assuredly, I say to you, whatever you bind on earth will be bound in heaven, and whatever you loose on earth will be loosed in heaven. Again I say to you that if two of you agree on earth concerning anything that they ask, it will be done for them by My Father in heaven." (Matthew 18:18-19 NKJV)

Have you ever wondered why God would give in to the will of men even when He didn't agree with their wishes? It is because the mirror binds Heaven and Earth. God did not want a high priest over His people. He wanted to speak to them directly but because they asked for that system, He gave it to them. God never wanted the Children of Israel to have a king over them but they asked for it so He gave it to them. This is as a direct result of the most powerful gift that God gave to man: a Will. A will is what makes us like God. Will literally means 'desire'. When you say 'I will open a business', you are saying that it is your desire to open a business. The wonderful thing, though, is that God gives you the desire of your heart (Psalm 37:4). Our will, however, is supposed to line up with the will of God. When it does, Earth and Heaven are in a state of synchronicity. When your life is in sync, then the Kingdom of God is alive in you. When your life lines up with the mirror, miracles happen. Mirror and Miracle are from the same root word, which means to 'look at'. Miracle means to 'look at in wonder'.

I challenge you today to become an original copy. The root of the word 'original' is 'origin'. What is your origin? Do not copy others. Become an original copy of the Father. Even more important than a name or a title is the relationship. Hence we can now call Him Father. We lost the Father-son relationship in the Garden. We also lost our warrantee and connection to the Maker. Jesus brought back our right to be His sons and to call Him Father again.

For many of us, the mirror is still broken or distorted. However, I have some good news. Your mirror can be repaired. You can repair this mirror by restoring your relationship with the Father; by restoring your true identity and reestablishing your true and rightful state of sonship. The answer is simple: Do the will of the Father. Jesus said that His mother and brothers are those who do the will of the Father. If you want to be a co-heir with Christ to the most powerful Kingdom on Earth, if you want to be entitled to the keys of the Kingdom of Heaven, then find the will of the Father for your life. Find your purpose and live it unwaveringly and to the fullest. With Vision, On Mission, In Purpose you are a son of the Most High God.

When the Man and the Mirror Don't Match

> "Not every one that saith unto me, Lord, Lord, shall enter into the kingdom of heaven; but he that **doeth the will** of my Father which is in heaven. Many will say to me in that day, Lord, Lord, have we not prophesied in thy name? and in thy name have cast out devils? and in thy name done many wonderful works? And then will I profess unto them, I never knew you: depart from me, ye that work iniquity." (Matthew 7:21-23 KJV)

I am sure that every single person reading this has stood in front of a mirror. Mirrors have become essential to our daily routine. Likewise, many of you have either been to a Hall of Mirrors at a carnival or circus or you have seen one on television. If you have, then you know what it is like to look into a mirror that works properly and you know what it is like to look into a distorted mirror. Distorted mirrors are actually curved mirrors that reflect distorted images. So, in essence, you look totally different from the image before you. This would be fun to look at if you were at a carnival, but it would be frustrating and useless if you were trying to get dressed for work.

When the man and the mirror don't match, the result is distortion. When you (the image) don't match with the mirror (the source), the result is iniquity. It is accepted that sin means 'to miss the mark'. So if the mark is for the image (you) to perfectly reflect the source then you fail if both sides don't line up. If the source is smiling but you are frowning then you have missed the mark. If the source is dressed as a doctor but you are dressed as a farmer then you have missed the mark. So 'sin' has to do with the act but iniquity has to do with the state. Iniquity is from the Hebrew word *avon* (Strongs 5771). It speaks to the state you are in as a result of sin, including a state of guilt.

Avon has been described as to bend, twist, or distort. This is exactly what is happening when the mirror images don't match up. But the Latin definition of iniquity is even more striking. Iniquity is from the Latin word *iniquus* which is comprised of *in*, which means 'not', and *iquus*, which means 'equal'. Iniquity, therefore, means 'not equal'. Therefore when Earth does not line up with or is not equal to Heaven, it is in a state of iniquity. When you do not line up with the Maker, the result is iniquity. Likewise when your life does not line up with the vision God has for your life, it amounts to iniquity. Vision is the image of yourself and your circumstances in the future that God created for you in the past. I again submit to you that the best way to determine if God knows you is to determine if you know yourself. If you don't know yourself then God doesn't know you either.

In the end, when you stand before the Maker, if you do not look like the image in the vision then you have missed the mark. In the end Christ says that you will stand before Him. I submit to you that Christ is the Great Mirror you will stand before. If your image is not equal to what it should be then you have failed. You may say, "I have cast out demons and healed the sick in your name" but He will say, "Depart from me, I do not know you." He does not recognize you because you do not match what you are supposed to be. Your life and your circumstances do not line up with the vision that God had for your life before you were in your mother's womb.

When you look in the mirror today, what do you see? Do you look like your vision? Are you headed in the direction of your vision? Are you in iniquity? Are you a distorted vision of your former self? Have you fallen into distraction? Are you a successful failure? If you answered 'yes' to any of these questions then you are in need of restoration. As we have learned, the problem is not a physical one, it is a mental one. What you are suffering from is a mental disease and therefore the solution is simple. All it requires is the renewing of your mind. *Meta Noeo*!

The Mirror Principle

God's ways will always be a mystery to man. However, while we may never really fully understand the mysteries of God we can definitely observe and admire the way He does things. For 20 years I have done just that, and time and again it has led me to one special discovery. That God constantly utilizes the principle of mirrors. Almost everything in the Bible reflects this powerful principle. So what does this mean? It is the principle upon which the Kingdom is based. The principle that there is a source and a reflection of that source; of the infinite, multiplying and omnipotent power that is manifested when two become one. There are so many biblical examples of this principle in action:

- Man is from God and is the mirror image of God.
- Man is also from the earth and is the mirror image of the earth. In fact man's entire make-up is similar to the earth's. For example, both man and the earth are made up of 70 percent water. Man was made from the earth and is made up of the same six main materials: nitrogen, oxygen, carbon, hydrogen, phosphorus and calcium. These, among others, are the main elements that constitute the earth.
- Woman is from man and is the mirror image of man.
- Children are from parents and are the mirror image of the parents.
- Marriage between a man and woman is the mirror image of the marriage between God and man, and Christ and the church. This is why adultery is the same as idolatry. They are both from the same word, *Pornos*.
- Earth is the replica of Heaven (that was the original intent).
- Abraham's sacrifice (attempted) of his son was the mirror image of God sacrificing His Son.
- The practice of sacrificing under the law was the mirror image of God's Son who would be sacrificed.
- John the Baptist was the mirror image of Elijah:
  - "For all the Prophets and the Law prophesied until John. And if you are willing to accept it, he is the Elijah who was to come." (Matthew 11:14 NKJV)
- Moses was the mirror image of Jesus.
- Moses prophesied: "A Prophet like me from your midst, from your brethren. Him you shall hear... And the Lord said to me: I will raise up for them a Prophet like you from among their brethren, and will put My words in His mouth, and He shall speak to them all that I command Him. And it shall be that whoever will not hear My words, which He speaks in My name, I will require it of him" (Deuteronomy 18:15,18-19 NKJV).
  - Both Jesus and Moses were born into great empires under the rule of a powerful emperor who was created just before their birth.

        - Egypt/Pharaoh: Joseph consolidated Pharaoh's power.
        - Rome/Caesar Augustus: Julius Caesar took Rome from a republic to a dictatorship. It was for this reason that he was killed, but Caesar Augustus carried on his rule.
    - All baby boys were ordered to be killed when both Jesus and Moses were born. Both escaped to Egypt from those who wanted to kill them.
    - Both spoke to God directly.
    - Both taught a new truth from God.
    - Both performed great miracles. Ironically the words 'mirror' and 'miracle' are from the same root word, meaning 'to look at in amazement'.
    - Moses turned water to blood: Jesus turned water to wine.
    - Both had control over wind and water: Moses parted the water and Jesus spoke to the water, calming it.
    - Moses walked through the water on dry land. Jesus walked on the water.
    - Both healed the sick.
    - Both healed lepers.
    - Both miraculously fed the multitudes.
    - Both were tested in the same wilderness: Moses for 40 years; Jesus for 40 days.
    - Both fasted for 40 days.
    - Moses could have been one of the rulers in the house of Pharaoh. Jesus was offered rulership by Satan.
    - Both were deliverers of the people.
    - Moses placed a serpent on a stick to heal the people. Jesus became 'the serpent on a stick' when our sins were placed on Him on the cross.
    - Moses' Passover, where the lamb's blood on persons' houses saved them from death, was the mirror image of Jesus' blood saving us from death.
    - Both were fugitives of the law.
    - Moses struck the rock to release the water: Jesus was the Rock that was struck, releasing living waters.
    - Neither would go to the Promised Land. Both would die so that their people could enter the Promised Land.
    - Both died on a hill.

- There was a confrontation in Heaven after both of their deaths between Michael the Angel and Satan.
- Neither of their bodies remained in a tomb.
- Their generation rebelled against them both and died as a result. The Children of Israel died in the wilderness, and Jesus' generation died in the great siege on Jerusalem in 70 AD.
- Their faces shined with the glory of Heaven: Jesus on the Mount of Transfiguration and Moses on Mount Sinai.
- Moses appointed 70 rulers over the people: Jesus anointed 70 disciples to teach the nations.
- Moses sent 12 spies into the Promised Land: Jesus sent 12 disciples out into the world.

> "Then those men, when they had seen the sign that Jesus did, said, 'This is truly the Prophet who is to come into the world.'" (John 6:14)

There are many more examples, but certainly from the exhaustive list above you can see that the lives of Moses and Jesus clearly mirrored each other. The mirror principle is a principle established and utilized by God and it is a powerful principle to apply to your life. Jesus made its application clear. If you want to be forgiven by God in Heaven then you must forgive your fellow man here on Earth. He said you show love for God, who you can't see, by showing love for your fellow man, who you can see. Judge not, and you shall not be judged. Condemn not, and you shall not be condemned. **Forgive**, and you will be **forgive**n. This is the powerful secret of the principle of the mirror: Whatever you do will be mirrored.

Again I ask, when you look in the mirror what do you see? If you don't see the Father then your mirror is broken. If you don't see the person God intended you to be then your mirror is distorted: the mirror of your mind, that is. You are in need of repentance: the renewing of your mind; the renewing of your life's mission and purpose – *Meta Noeo*. Are you in need of a transformation? Are you in need of a miracle in your life? When your life lines up with the mirror, that is when you are connected. That is when you are able to tap into the power of Heaven. That is when you have access to all of the protection and provision of the Kingdom of God. That is when Mir-acles happen. That is when what you bind on Earth is bound in Heaven. That is when what you loose on Earth is loosed in Heaven.

The Secrets

- Man's crisis is an identity crisis. Man has forgotten who he is, both personally and collectively.
- Because man doesn't know who he is, the result is that he abuses himself and those around him.
- When you are looking with spiritual eyes, physical appearance and attributes mean little to you. You are able to see through the outer skin directly into the soul and source of man.
- Our identity is predicated upon our ability to be like God.
- We are the reflection of God and Earth is a reflection of Heaven. The first duty of the image is to do the will of the other side.
- The secret is that the mirror works both ways!
- When your life lines up with the mirror, miracles happen.
- When the man and the mirror don't match, the result is distortion.
- Sin has to do with the act, but iniquity has to do with the state.
- When you do not line up with the Maker, the result is iniquity.
- The best way to determine if God knows you is to determine if you know yourself. If you don't know yourself then God doesn't know you either.
- God constantly utilizes the principle of mirrors.
- Whatever you do will be mirrored.

Chapter 7: AM-nesia

He woke up suddenly, surrounded by darkness and the sounds of panic and commotion.

"Somebody help him!" a voice screamed in terror.
"The door is jammed!" another frantic voice said.

His head was wet with a liquid that began draining down his forehead and into his eyes. It was blood. It was draining heavily. He attempted to lift his arm to wipe his eyes but he couldn't: The pain was excruciating. He was pinned down. But he was not alone. Faint and too weak to fight, he heard someone struggling in front of him.

"Don't worry, sir. I'll get you out," the voice said.

He heard the door of a car open and the person in front got out. He realized that he was trapped in the back seat of a mangled car, the victim of a violent car accident. He faded in and out of consciousness until he heard the loud crash of glass next to his head. Someone grabbed him by his armpits, pulled him through the window and laid him on the ground. The person took a handkerchief and gently wiped the blood from his eyes. When he opened them, he could see the man who had pulled him out bending over him: an extremely old man but sharply dressed in a now bloodied suit.

"You're safe," the old man said. "The ambulance is on the way."

As he heard those words he fell unconscious.

He awoke to the sounds of beeping machines all around him. He took a few seconds to adjust his eyes to the light. He was wearing a blue hospital gown and was wired to the beeping machines. In the corner of the room, asleep in a chair next to the window, was the old man who had pulled him from the wreckage. A nurse happened to walk into the room to check on him and saw that he was awake. The nurse rushed to his bedside.

"How do you feel?" she asked.

He didn't answer.

"What's your name?" the nurse asked.

He again didn't answer. He looked around the room as if confused.

"Where am I?" he asked.

"You're in the hospital. You were in a car accident three days ago. Now, do you remember your name? Who are you?"

He stared at the nurse, then at the old man asleep in the corner of the room.

"I, I, I, I don't know." It was a confusing, empty feeling. A terrifying feeling, like dreaming you are falling in the dark.

"Oh dear," the nurse said with a tone of concern in her voice. "I have to call the doctor right way."

She scurried out the door, which slammed shut behind her. It woke the old man.

"You're back," he said joyfully as he struggled to his feet.

The nurse hustled back into the room with a doctor in tow. They rushed to his bedside. The doctor checked his vitals. They were good.

"Who are you?" the doctor asked.

"I don't know..." he replied, the confusion evident on his face. It was like waking from a dream and not remembering what you had dreamt. You know you had a dream; the dream was so real. But you just can't remember what you dreamt.

"Who is this gentleman standing next to you?" the doctor asked.

He stared up at the only familiar face in the room. The old man smiled at him gently, patiently awaiting his answer.

"I don't know him," he said. He could remember his face from the scene of the accident but did not know him otherwise.

The old man looked shocked. "You don't remember me?" he said pleadingly. "I'm Mr Adams. Do you remember?"

But he only stared blankly at the old man. On his wrist was a nametag. It read 'John Doe', the interim name they had put on the tag in order to have him registered.

"I'm your boss, Mr Adams. You've been my loyal employee for six years now."

"Your employee?" he replied. "What kind of employee? What do I do?"

"Young man, you're my Gardener. I live on a large estate in the suburbs. I hired you six years ago to till my lawn and Garden."

Nothing the old man said was familiar to him, but he did fit the bill of a wealthy employer. He wore an expensive suit and he smelled of expensive cologne. The pen in his pocket was a designer pen and the watch on his wrist was definitely worth a fortune. He was relieved to know who he was, but he still did not have the comfort of the memories that go along with life's journeys. It was an empty feeling.

"What happened?" he asked. "You were driving me. Where were we going? Why was I in the back seat of your car?"

"I was taking you home to your apartment as I sometimes do when you work late. I stopped at the traffic lights and without warning a semi-truck smashed into us from behind. I was unharmed and managed to get out of the car, and I pulled you out of the back seat. You always sit in the back seat. It's a habit of yours."

"What about my family? My mother, my father, my wife, my children? Where am I from?"

"I don't know your family. You live in a one-bedroom apartment. I've never heard you talk about family in the six years you've worked for me. But I did retrieve your cell phone from the car. It should have all your contacts in it… if you can remember the password to unlock it."

The next day the old man checked him out of the hospital and, as a kind gesture, allowed him to stay in his guesthouse, located in the mansion's backyard. His recovery was quick. Within a week or so he was back to work tending to the yard around the mansion – always around the mansion but never inside it. He was forbidden to go inside. He worked diligently, even doing repairs around the estate. It was amazing that he could remember how to do plumbing and electrical work but could not remember how or where he had learned it or who had taught him. Then the flashes began – the memory flashes. Images would flash into his head; he would see memories of himself in the back seat being driven home by Mr Adams. He would also see images of people he did not know. Who were these people?

One day he was sitting on a rock in the yard taking a break from his labors when suddenly the back door began to open slowly. Out popped the head of an old lady dressed in some kind of uniform. She had a strange hat on her head. She carefully and cautiously looked around as if to make sure no one was around. When she was satisfied that it was all clear, she hurried over to him.

"Good morning," he said extending his hand for a handshake.

"Be quiet!" the woman replied in a strong whisper. "I'm the cook in the main house. I was told not to communicate with you. But something is terribly wrong here. Something is terribly wrong with this picture."

"What do you mean?" he replied, getting to his feet.

"They said you're suffering from amnesia and that you should be allowed to come back to yourself without assistance; otherwise it could harm you psychologically."

"It must be working. I'm remembering how to build and repair things," he said enthusiastically. "And I can see memory flashes of being in the back of the car."

"Is that all you see?" the woman replied.

"No. I see images of people I don't know."

The old lady pushed her hand into a large side pocket in her dress and pulled out a hand mirror. "Maybe this might help," she said as she placed it in his hand.

He was confused as to how a mirror might help him in the state he was in, but he decided to be polite and accept it. Besides, there were no mirrors in the guesthouse and he had not seen himself since the accident. The woman turned to walk away then remembered she had something else in her other pocket. From it she retrieved a small cell phone.

"The old man kept it from you. It's been ringing constantly every day. Someone out there is trying desperately to reach you!" The lady turned and hurried back into the house without another word.

With the mirror in one hand and the cell phone in the other, he paced back and forth in the backyard concentrating with all his might, trying to remember the password for the cell phone or hoping that it would ring. After what seemed like hours of pacing he sat on the rock again. Tired and frustrated, he dropped the mirror and phone to the ground in front of him. He stared into the distance for a few more minutes then threw his head on his knees in frustration. Then he saw his reflection. The mirror had landed face up between his feet and he found himself staring straight into it. He was face-to-face with himself and the image looked so familiar. Then a moment of enlightenment overwhelmed him. The image he was looking at was so much like the images of the people he had been seeing in his memory. There was no mistaking it; these familiar faces were definitely family. Those two words, he thought, are so deeply rooted in each other: 'Familiar'; 'family'. His excitement started to build. How would he find them? Where could they be? Were they even alive?

He picked up the mirror and realized that there was a tiny inscription on the handle. It read 'DOMINION'. The same inscription was on a plaque on the gate at the entrance of the house. He picked up his cell phone and opened the screen. 'Enter your password' it said. Instinctively he typed in the eight-letter word 'DOMINION'. Access was granted. He was beside himself with joy. Immediately he went to his contact list. There were so many people. Who should he call? Who would know him? Then as he scrolled down, he saw a familiar word that warmed and woke him up like morning coffee: 'Father'. At the same moment he saw the name, the phone began to ring in his hand, startling him to the point that he almost dropped it. The caller ID said 'Father'. After a few rings he built up the courage to answer it.

"Hello?" he said cautiously.

"Hello," the voice replied.

"Is this… are you my father?"

"I am."

He welled up with emotion and broke down in tears at the confirmation.

"Where are you?" his father asked.

"I'm not sure. I work the yard at a house called Dominion. It belongs to a kind man called Mr Adams."

His father went silent.

"Father, are you there?"

"My son," his father replied gently, "you are Mr Adams."

He jumped to his feet in shock. The phone slipped from his hand and fell onto the rock, shattering it into pieces. He gazed up at the back door of the house and started to walk towards it. Memories began to flood into his head. When he reached the back door he turned the knob and the door opened. He entered into the beautiful mansion. There were people inside laughing and having fun, and most of them looked like him. On the walls were large portraits. None of the portraits were of the old man, Mr Adams. They resembled the images of the people he had seen in his memories. His father, his mother, himself…

Identity Theft

The parable you have just read is as real as could be. It is the story of mankind – the story of the greatest tragedy of mankind. It is the story of mankind's tragic accident in the beginning that led to the most notorious incident of identity theft in history. This grand larceny resulted in all of the major problems we face today, personally and collectively. The issue for many people is how can they be all that they can be when they don't know what they are supposed to be? How can we be all that we can be when we don't know who we are? Well, now that we know who we are, now that we know that we are sons of God, the question is what is a son of God and what can a son of God do?

We learned in Chapter 1 that the enemy's primary goal was to get us out of Eden and take control of our dominion. He accomplished this by stealing our identity. He stole our identity by getting us to forget who we are. When we were disconnected from God we lost our spiritual sight. The mirror was broken and we could no longer see our true selves. We could no longer see who we truly are. As a result we were stuck with the only side of ourselves that we could see: our physical selves. This led us on a long, misguided journey to find out who we are and where we came from.

The search for our source led us to worship seemingly powerful things around us. We began to worship the sun, the moon and the animals. We went even further and created gods from wood, stone and metal to worship. That still left many with an unfulfilled void. So we began a search for our source that didn't include the worship of any deity. Over time, this led to the birth of the theory of evolution. Existence by itself, by accident, and we evolved from the animals that resulted from that accident. In essence, we evolved from some ape-like creature. This is not to argue against the theory of evolution. It is up to you to believe what you will believe. However, I have come to the understanding that the son of a monkey is a monkey. A monkey cannot beget a cat, nor can it beget a human. I think that all of these theories have come about as a result of the loss of our true identity. We should not be worshiping things and animals. They should be serving us. God gave man Earth and everything on it and gave us dominion over them: over the sea, the land, the air and the cosmos, and everything in them. We lost our identity and started worshiping the things that we were given dominion over and started to see them as our source instead of seeing God as our true source. As in the story above, we became the servant in our own house. Satan took rulership of our home and we became servants. However, despite the fact that we were playing the role of servants, in truth we were still truly the owners of the estate. The problem wasn't that we were servants; the problem was that we didn't know who we truly were. This is the true tragedy of us all. Your true tragedy is not your dead-end job. Your true tragedy is that you have no idea what you truly are or what you should be doing. You are suffering from the greatest crisis of them all: Identity Crisis.

Are We Really Ambassadors?

There is one title and role that we seem to have universally accepted. That is the title of ambassadors. Us church folks have generally accepted that we are ambassadors for Christ. In fact, Paul spoke about it twice:

> "Now then, we are ambassadors for Christ, as though God were pleading through us: we implore *you* on Christ's behalf, be reconciled to God." (2 Corinthians 5:20 NKJV)

> "...and for me, that utterance may be given to me, that I may open my mouth boldly to make known the mystery of the gospel, for which I am an *ambassador in chains*; that in it I may speak boldly, as I ought to speak". (Ephesians 6:19-20 NKJV)

When Paul made these statements, what exactly did he mean by 'ambassador'? What is an ambassador? The Latin word for ambassador is *ambactus* which means 'servant'. An ambassador in Paul's day was a servant of the king. His role was primarily to be a messenger of the king, unlike today where ambassadors represent the nation and not the head of state. There were no instant communication methods in those days as there are today. Therefore the king used ambassadors to deliver his messages to other heads of state. Due to the fact that delivering the king's message was such a critically important role, it could only be entrusted to the most loyal, dependable and trusted servant. Therefore, servants chosen to be ambassadors were mature, elderly men selected for their wisdom. This was important because sometimes critical decisions had to be made independently on behalf of the king. This was even more critical in situations where ambassadors were called on to take up residence in important trading states to represent the king's interest.

Interestingly, the Greek meaning of the name 'Paul', used in the first scripture above (2 Corinthians 5:20), is 'elder' (*Presbeuó*: to be the elder, to take precedence). So, in other words, Paul was saying to the Corinthians that he and his fellow men were the respected and trusted servant messengers of Christ. That the words he was speaking to them were not his words but were spoken on behalf of Christ. In the second scripture above (Ephesians 6:20), Paul referred to himself as an ambassador in chains. He was metaphorically saying that he was a servant in chains, bonded as a messenger for Christ.

What Paul is saying is so true. We have a duty to be messengers for Christ. However, there is more to who we are than servant messengers. WARNING: What I am about to reveal to you will change your consciousness, challenge your religion, and cause a paradigm shift in your life. What I am about to say to you will lead to the renewing of your mind and result in abundant life. If you are comfortable with your life thus far and would prefer to remain in your comfort zone, you have no need to read any further. However, if your soul is unsatisfied, if your spirit is telling you that there is something about you that you don't quite understand yet, if you truly want to understand what you are and what you can do, then read on.

We Are Not Just Ambassadors!

For us, 'ambassador' is a role not a title. Being a servant messenger is something you do as a part of who you are. To call yourself an ambassador is like saying Steve Jobs was a father, or Bill Gates is a husband, or that Oprah is a great-auntie. It's like saying your mother is a cook because she cooks you breakfast and dinner. It's like saying your dad is a driver because he drives you to school. Technically, Steve Jobs was a father but was that truly all that he was? Is that what history will remember him as? Truly, your mother is a cook. She does cook you breakfast and dinner but that is just a role she carries out because of what she truly is: a mother. If you started referring to your mother as 'the cook' that would not be very nice. When your dad pulls up to pick you up from school, you would not say, "The driver is here." When you get in the car you would not say, "Good afternoon, driver." Ambassador or servant messenger is a role we carry out because of who we are, but it is not who we are. Let's look at the characteristics of an ambassador:

- They are servants of the king.
- They are messengers of the king.
- They are representatives of the king.
- They own nothing around them.
    - The car, the house, the phone, even the bed they sleep in, belongs to the king.
- They have immunity in the place they are serving but they have no power there.
- They do not rule anyone or anything.
- They cannot make laws.
- They cannot arrest anyone.
- They are not sent to work or become anything.

The role of being a servant messenger for God is an honorable one indeed. We must speak what the Lord says and spread the good news of His Kingdom. It is a role that you must carry out every day of your life tirelessly, without ceasing. However, it is a role not a title. It is a job description not a job. So then, what are we? I submit to you that we are not ambassadors. Angels are the ambassadors of God. They are His messengers. They are His servant messengers. The word 'angel' means 'messenger' (from the Latin, *angelus*). They come to us from the presence of God to represent God: "I am **Gabriel**, who stands in the presence of God, and was sent to speak to you and bring you these glad tidings" (Luke 1:19). Ambassadors are foreigners just as angels are foreigners on Earth. We are not foreigners on Earth. We are literally sons of the soil. Earth is our realm and here we have dominion. Therefore, angels are clearly ambassadors; it is not just something they do, it is what they are. So if angels are messengers then what are we?

> "So you are no longer a slave, but God's child; and since you are his child, God has made you also an heir." (Galatians 4:7 NIV)

What is it that God has that we are heirs to? The answer is simple: the Kingdom! The son of the King is not a servant. The son of the King is a king! The son of the King is not an ambassador. The son of the King is a king. We are kings sent out by the King to rule our dominion. We rule our dominion and He rules us.

Dominion

God never intended man to be servant messengers. To understand this we must go back to God's original intent. When God made Adam He did not make him to be a servant messenger. When God made man He made him in His image and likeness, like a son is made in the image and likeness of a father, and He gave man dominion over all the Earth.

"Then God said, 'Let Us make man in our image, according to our likeness; let them have dominion over the fish of the sea, over the birds of the air, and over the cattle, over all the earth and over every creeping thing that creeps on the earth.' So God created man in His *own* image; in the image of God He created him; male and female He created them. Then God blessed them, and God said to them, "Be fruitful and multiply; fill the earth and subdue it; have dominion over the fish of the sea, over the birds of the air, and over every living thing that moves on the earth."(Genesis 1:26-28 NKJV)

God made man to have dominion. Ambassadors have no dominion. Listen, words are very powerful. When you say "I am going to cook" those words impact on your actions. When you say "You are a cook" it impacts on who you are. Why take a title that is based on one of your roles in life when you can take a title that is based on who you are and where you are from? Christ is the King of kings, not the King of messengers. Yes, a king has messengers and Christ has messengers but that is not the good news; that is not the Gospel. The king hiring a servant is not newsworthy. But the king having a son would make news worldwide. When America sends its ambassadors out to different countries, it doesn't make the headlines in America. No one cares. But if the Prince of England is having a son, the world is watching!

The good news is that you are the son of the King: The heir to the throne and a co-heir with Christ. The word 'king' is derived from the word 'kin'. As in 'next of kin'. Simply put: 'family'. This is why our family relationship to God and Christ is stressed so much in the new covenant. We are family and heirs! When you are an heir to the King, the following is your inheritance:

- Ownership
  - Kings have ownership and dominion.
    - The word Lord means 'owner'.
    - Hence we call Christ the 'Lord of lords': The Owner of owners.
  - Ambassadors own nothing.
- Dominion
  - Kings rule their domain.
  - Ambassadors rule nothing.
- Power
  - Kings have power.
    - They can decree and declare.
    - They can bind and loose whomsoever they please.
      - "Assuredly, I say to you, whatever you **bind** on earth will be bound in heaven, and whatever you loose on earth will be loosed in heaven."(Matthew 18:18 NKJV)
  - Ambassadors have no power.
    - They cannot make decrees.
    - They cannot bind or loose anyone. They cannot arrest or free a person.
- Territory
  - Kings have defined territories.
    - Kings live in a palace or mansion (the chief residence of a lord).
    - "In my Father's house are many **mansions**: if it were not so, I would have told you. I go to prepare a place for you" (John 14:2 NKJV). He did not go to prepare an embassy.
  - Ambassadors have no territory.

To put it in perspective, you are a king under the King. The King you are under is the King of kings. In the time when Jesus spoke of the 'King of kings', this was a literal term clearly understood in His day. For example, King Herod was the king in Jesus' day. However, he was under a 'king' of the kings, who was the emperor Caesar Augustus. Herod was given dominion over most of Israel, including Judea, Galilee, Batanaea, and Perea. Other kings were given dominion over other areas of the empire but they all came under the main king who ruled the entire empire. The smaller kings were sent out to represent the big king. Even though they were sent out by him to do his will, they were not considered ambassadors – they were royalty. Yes, their role is similar to that of ambassadors in some ways; however, they have something ambassadors don't, and that is dominion. A smaller king can do as he pleases in his domain. He can arrest or free persons. He can even make laws and decrees. However, the big king is in control and can make laws to override the small kings if he pleases.

This same system exists today even in democracies. The President of the United States is the 'big king'. The governors of the states are the 'small kings'. Governors have dominion over their state. They can arrest or pardon people and they can sign bills into law. However, the federal government is bigger and the President has the power to sign federal laws that supersede local laws. As explained earlier, when Jesus said to Peter that this information was 'given to you directly from Heaven and not from any man, and that this is the rock upon which I will build my church', this system is what Jesus was referring to: The Kingdom of kings. Kings who got their instructions directly from the big king and who carried out his will. As explained earlier, church was a secular word. It meant the assembly or the council. The smaller kings were a part of a special council that answered to and carried out the will of the bigger king. They were sent out, as such, to their domains. The difference between them and ambassadors is that ambassadors go to a strange and foreign land of which they are not a citizen and which is the domain of someone else. When a king is assigned to a domain, it is not a foreign land; it is a part of the empire. Angels are ambassadors because they are not from Earth, nor do they belong on Earth. The dominion of Earth belongs to man and so angels fit the symbolism of ambassadors perfectly.

You are a king and governor. The domain to which you are assigned is not foreign land. It is not the domain of anyone else. It is *your* domain. You were given dominion by the King of kings and Lord of lords. The original intent for God making Earth and putting man in it was to expand the Kingdom of Heaven on Earth. The intent of the Kingdom is colonization. The Kingdom doesn't send an ambassador to the place he has colonized; he sends a governor! He doesn't set up an embassy in the colony; he sets up a governor's mansion. That is why you are here, in this domain with dominion.

The enemy's goal is to steal your identity by making you forget who you truly are. He wants to make you like him instead of like God. Satan is an angel; he wants you to take on his image instead of taking on the image of your true Father, the King. For if you don't know that you are a son of the King and if you don't know what that entitles you to, then he can steal it from you.

Domain

Now that you know what you are, the only question that remains is: What can I do? The answer is, the only thing that kings do – dominate! Every king has dominion and all dominion is confined to a domain. The key for every king is to find their domain. Your domain is the realm in which you were called to exist. It is not necessarily a physical realm but rather it is the realm of your calling. It is the realm within your purpose. Purpose sets a boundary which defines your mission. That mission is the Way. That mission is your Way. Your Way is your domain.

The perfect illustration of domain in the Bible is the Garden of Eden. When you search for the meaning of 'Eden', what you find is a group of descriptions that describe a concept. As mentioned previously, what you find is that Eden is the 'spot'; the place where there is a connection to God; it is a fruitful and pleasurable place. Practically speaking, Eden is that place where you were placed to do your work and it is the work you were placed there to do. When you do anything outside of that place, you are out of place. You are a trespasser. This is why Jesus referred to sins as trespasses when He taught us the Lord's Prayer. In that 'spot' you are entitled to and enjoy full and direct connection with God. Outside of that place you are disconnected and lost. In that place all of your efforts are fruitful and blessed. Outside of that place your efforts are laborious and fruitless. Your domain is the only place in which you will find true and lasting pleasure. The key is to find your spot.

As mentioned earlier, a recent Gallup Poll has revealed that 70 percent of Americans hate their jobs. In the Gospel of Thomas there is a very powerful statement attributed to Jesus. It says: "Don't do what you hate!" Most people get jobs for the wrong reasons. They choose a job because they will make a lot of money. Some choose a job because it will give them stature in society. However, the key to choosing your career is not to do what you would do for money but rather choose that thing that you would do for free. Choose the thing that you love: That thing that you would do for free just because you love it. Your work is your worship carried out in your world. It determines your worth and makes you worthy.

Dominion is an action word: 'Do-minion'. It is the place where you do your work. Likewise, 'dominate' is an action word. Ironically, 'king' is also an action word: Hence the 'ing' in the word 'king'. The letters 'ING' are in every word that describes what you do. Hence, in every action is the opportunity to be a 'KING', and every action is the expression of a king. Whether you are sing-ing, danc-ing, speak-ing, build-ing, draw-ing, no matter what you are do-ing, if you are wor-king in your domain then you are a king. Jesus said, "I confer on you a Kingdom just as the Father conferred one on me" (Luke 22:29). A kingdom is the domain of a king: King-dom. In your domain there is: Power, Protection, Provision, and Presence.

In your domain you will find the source of unlimited power. As in the Michael Jordan story you read about earlier, you may be disconnected from everything else you do but find that there is one thing that enables you to tap into power beyond human comprehension. In your domain you will find ultimate protection. In the Bible, Job was covered by a hedge of protection that no man, no angel, and not even the devil could penetrate. As long as you are in your purpose, in your mission, you are protected. As long as you are in your Way, on your Way, you are unstoppable. This does not mean that bad things will not happen. It means that bad things will not stop you.

It was Paul's mission to go to Rome and speak to King Agrippa. On his way there he was beaten up by a mob of Jews and arrested. His Roman citizenship entitled him to a hearing in Rome before the king. On the way he experienced a shipwreck. He was able to comfort everyone on the ship by telling them they would live. This is because he was protected by purpose and therefore if they stuck with him, they would live. When they got to dry land a deadly viper came out of a campfire and bit him and hung onto his hand. Those who witnessed it were sure that he must have been an evil man because even after escaping the shipwreck, justice was not letting him escape alive. Paul simply shook the snake off in the fire and continued doing what he was doing. The snakebite had no effect on him. So protection is like a bullet-proof vest. It doesn't mean you won't get shot; it means you won't get stopped. In my life I have miraculously survived so many life-threatening situations that each one emboldened me to know that I am here for a purpose greater than my own selfish desires.

Whatever your dream, if it is within your domain, the provisions are there for it already. Many people use the lack of money as an excuse for not fulfilling their dreams. Either they say that they don't have the money to start the business or endeavor, or they have the excuse that they can't quit their job to pursue their dreams because they have too many bills and a family to take care of. They are no different from the man who failed to use his one talent and, like him, they will find themselves in outer darkness.

Here is a great secret. If you understand this, you will never let this excuse hold you back again. The secret is that money isn't real. Why are you stressing over something that bankers can just print out as they please? The secret is that as long as you have something that someone else wants, then you have money. That is the secret of value. The key is not to wait for money, neither is it to look for money. The key is to make yourself valuable. Your gift makes you valuable. When you are valuable you become important. When you are important people will import you. It is that simple. Your work determines your worth! You are a walking money magnet. Your work activates your magnetism. So don't focus on money first. First focus on your gift and your gift will attract the provision.

Sometime around the year 2000, my gospel-singing quartet named Vision had dreams of traveling around the world to sing. We were all young men with a vision but no provision to fulfill our dreams, nor did we have the opportunity or a platform. By this time we had already won multiple awards and were well known in our country, but we wanted more. We wanted to minister to the world. We decided to get back into the studio and record another song. I was in college in Florida at the time and had to fly back to the Bahamas for a day to record the song. I flew in and we went to the studio to record the song. The engineer heard it and immediately said he didn't like it. He said it sounded great but it was not the one. He asked if we had another song. We said we had another song but we didn't have time to practice it because I had to travel back to school the next day. He insisted that we let him hear the song. We had not practiced or sung the song at all for five years but when we sang it for him he loved it. "Go in the booth! Let's record it," he insisted. So we did. It was beautiful. It was amazing that we had not practiced this song for five years and yet it just worked. One shot – one take. There was definitely something greater than us in control.

The song was written before I was born. I had never heard it before we practiced it for the first time five years earlier, and I had never gone back to it. It was written by a man who none of us knew personally, but we all knew of him. The song was 'Brand New World'. The man was Dr Myles Munroe. The song became our second national smash hit. It was playing on

Gospel and secular radio stations. Ironically, he wrote and performed the song when he was a part of a singing group called the Visionaires. When Dr Myles heard our rendition of the song he immediately summoned us to tell us how much he loved it. He told us that he wanted us to perform the song before he preached. We told him that we would love to perform at his church on Sunday.

"Not only at my church on Sunday," he gently responded, smiling, "I want you to perform before I preach around the world."

We couldn't believe how soon and how suddenly this door had opened for us. It was the beginning of a beautiful synergy and a beautiful relationship with a man who became like a father to me. Money for the trips poured in from sponsors and we got to fulfill our dream. I immediately dropped out of college and another member quit his job. The moral of this story is, where there is vision there is provision. We made our gift valuable by putting it in a great song and people began to import us. We traveled with Dr Myles, and independently, to North America, South America, the Caribbean, and Europe. We appeared on all the major Christian networks: TBN, The Word Network, BET, and INSP. We also appeared on local TV stations around the world. We were in our domain – connected and in the Presence. In this place we found unimaginable pleasure. In our domain! In our spot!

I invite you to find your domain. That thing that will bring you ultimate pleasure. That thing that you would drop everything else to do, because the Kingdom of God is like a man who finds a treasure and goes and sells everything he has to buy that treasure. I hereby declare Power, Protection, Provision, and the Presence of God in your life. I loose and activate all the hidden potential trapped inside you. I release you from the congregation of the dead and anoint you living kings under the power and authority of the King of kings. You are no longer a servant. You are a co-heir with Jesus Christ Himself. You are a son of the Living God. You are an heir to the mighty and powerful Kingdom of God. Take this revelation with you wherever you go. Keep it in your heart and remind yourself daily:

The Kingdom of God is the kingdom of gods!
Pass it on!

The Final Secrets

- The enemy's primary goal was to get us out of Eden and to take control of our dominion.
- He accomplished this by stealing our identity.
- He stole our identity by getting us to forget who we are.
- What is a son of God and what can a son of God do? A son of God is a king – a king has dominion!
- Idol worship and theories like evolution have come about as a result of the loss of our true identity.
- Your true tragedy is not your dead-end job. Your true tragedy is that you have no idea who you truly are or what you should be doing.
- For us, 'ambassador' is a role, not a title.
- Ambassador or servant messenger is a role we carry out because of who we are, but it is not who we are.
- We are not ambassadors. Angels are the ambassadors of God.
- What is it that God has that we are heirs to? The answer is simple: the Kingdom!
- The son of a King is not a servant. The son of a King is a king! The son of a King is not an ambassador. The son of a King is a king! When God made Adam He did not make him to be a servant messenger.
- God made man to have dominion.
- You are a king under the King. The King you are under is the King of kings.
- The intent of the Kingdom is colonization. The Kingdom doesn't send an ambassador to the place he has colonized; he sends a governor!
- The key for every king is to find their domain.
- Within your domain you are entitled to and can enjoy full and direct connection with God.
- Dominion is an action word: Do-minion. Domain is an action word. Dominate is an action word
- King is also an action word: Hence the 'ing' in the word 'king'. The letters 'ING' are in every word that describes what you do.
- Whatever your dream, if it is within your domain, the provisions are there for it already.
- The key is not to wait for money, neither is it to look for money. The key is to make yourself valuable. Your gift makes you valuable.

Made in the USA
Lexington, KY
27 January 2019